MESSIANIC PRAYERBOOK

2ND EDITION

(Revised - 2013)

RAY LOOKER

MESSIANIC PRAYER BOOK

(2nd Edition) Revised - 2013

All Scriptures are from the King James Bible

Author: Ray Looker
Website: http://www.raylooker.com
Email: raylooker@raylooker.com

ISBN-13: 978-1481130691
ISBN-10: 1481130692

BOOKS BY RAY LOOKER

Available: Amazon.com
(Paperback and Ebook)

Messianic Prayer Book, 2nd Ed

Messianic Code of Jewish Law

Amazing Gospel of Jesus

In Defense of Truth

Replacement Theology

Judeo-Christianity, 2nd Ed

Messianic Guide to the Epistles

Yahshua - The Messianic Hope

Suffering for Righteousness Sake

End-Time Prophecy

(http://www.raylooker.com)

PREFACE

In this second edition of "The Messianic Prayer Book", the writer is attempting to present a Messianic Prayer Book which gleans the richness of Jewish Liturgy with the Messianic Covenant brought to us with the coming of the Messiah Yahshua.

Yahweh's admonition to keep the Feasts and Festivals of Yahweh has not diminished, nor departed from the Scriptures, but are required even today of both Jewish and Christian Believers. While the admonition is there, in the past centuries as those who believed in the Messiah drifted further from Scripture, the means of how to observe these Festivals and Commandments of Yahweh has been forgotten and lost to Christian Believers in Yahshua as the Messiah.

The writer has attempted to reconcile both the admonition and the observance into a Messianic Prayer Book that allows all Believers in the Messiah to observe these Commandments in the knowledge that Yahshua is the fulfillment of the Feast and shares in the commemoration of the observance.

To those believers who have never been exposed to Jewish Liturgy, but are becoming more aware of our negligence in observing these Commandments of Yahweh, this Messianic Prayer Book will help them assume their rightful place in the required observance of these Feasts. Many Believers are falling away from the traditional church, and seeking a new identity. An identity which is focused upon the entire Scriptures, and requiring that we be observant of Yahweh's Commandments. The advantage of a private Prayer Book (Siddur) lends itself to family worship in the home rather than trying to adhere strictly with the local community of Believers in assemblies that seek denominational blessings at the expense of those who seek "something else".

Most Christian Holidays come to us from Babylonian religious practices. These "man-made" feasts claim to be Scriptural, but they are not. Their origins began in Babylon and Egypt. It is not the writer's point, within the context of this preface to chastise the conduct and behavior of any denomination, rather to offer those Jews and Christians who do not "fit-in", an opportunity to enter into a meaningful and time tested method of approaching Yahweh in a manner that is as old as time itself, in the home with their families, and with everyone participating within the family group.

The writer believes that the First Edition of this Prayer Book is the first time a Messianic Prayer Book of this nature has ever been prepared for publication. This Second Edition has been greatly expanded in breath and scope. The inclusion of transliterated Hebrew Blessings is designed to allow the reader to learn to pray the blessings in the Hebrew language.

The major emphasis of the Prayer Book is on family worship and the teaching of obedience to the Word of Yahweh to the next generation. The entire construct of this Prayer Book lends itself to increased family interaction, and quality time spent together in worship to Yahweh.

The order of worship begins with the Morning Blessings, and the Morning Prayer. This is followed by the AMIDAH, and the reading of Scriptures. The afternoon, MINCHAH Prayer is said, and in the evening there is the MAARIV Prayer and the Prayer for Retiring at Night

On Friday evening, and the evening before a High Holy Sabbath, which occurs on the first day of a major feast, a Sabbath Welcoming Service is held. This includes the Blessings for the lighting of the candles, the Sabbath Welcome, the KIDDUSH-the Blessings over the Bread and the Wine (Grape Juice is accepted) and the Blessings upon the wife, husband and the children.

Saturday morning includes the above daily services, as well as a service for the Blessings for the Sabbath. The Sabbath is ended in the evening with the HAVDALAH (the Sabbath Closing Prayer). In all cases, personal Prayer and songs of praise and adoration to Yahweh are encouraged to be added as the group is lead to worship Yahweh.

On the Festivals, i.e., New Moon [Rosh Kodesh], Passover [Pesach], Pentecost [Shavuot], New Year [Rosh Hashanah], Day of Atonement [Yom Kippur], Tabernacles [Sukkoth] , Lights and Dedication [Chanukah] and Deliverance [Purim], a special service is included in remembrance of what Yahweh has done for us on these Festivals in times past. The Jewish New Year Service [Rosh Hashanah] can be used as well for the December 31st/January 1st celebration. Once again, reminding us that a rededication of our lives to live more righteously for Yahweh is in line with our personal commitments to Yahweh for the New Year.

The Prayer of Penitence and Fasting (SELICHOT) should be said at every New Moon Festival as these are Minor days of Atonement, and many people will fast in some manner on these days as well.

SIMCHAT TORAH (the Eighth day of the Festival of Tabernacles-Sukkoth) is the day that the reading of the Books of the Law (the TORAH), are completed and a new reading begins. In the back of this Prayer Book is a listing of the "Torah Readings" for each week. Sometimes there are two Torah Readings which can only be known by getting a Jewish Calendar and cross checking the calendar with the Torah Reading for that week. SIMCHAT TORAH is also the day that Yahshua was circumcised and dedicated in the Temple. This symbolically indicates the ending of the "Old" and the beginning of the "New" Covenant of Yahweh with His people.

The presentation of this Prayer Book (Messianic Siddur) represents yet another milestone in the preparation for the coming of the Messiah. It has been my distinct privilege to have been used of my Heavenly Father in the preparation of this work.

My special thanks, blessings and praises to my wife Chianna, who has borne the burdens of sorrow and suffering with me, and has unselfishly supported and encouraged me every step of the way, I humbly offer praises and thanksgiving to the Most High for granting me this unique privilege of presenting this Prayer Book for your use in learning and observing how to keep the Festivals commanded by Yahweh.

Ray Looker-2005/2013

1 Tevet 5766/5773

CONTENTS

CONTENTS – Continue

CONTENTS – Continue

MORNING BLESSINGS

Blessed is Yahweh our God, King of the universe. I offer thanks to You living and eternal King, for You have mercifully restored my soul within me. Your faithfulness is great.

> [Baruch atah Adonai eloheinu, melech ha-Olam modeh ani L'fonecha, melech chai v'kayom, she-heche-zarto bi nishmosi b'chemlo raboh emunosecho.]

Blessed is Yahweh our God, King of the universe, who has sanctified us with Your commandments, and commanded us concerning the washing of the hands.

[Baruch atah Adonai eloheinu, melech ha-Olam Asher kid'shanu b'mitzvotav v'tzivanu al n'tilas yadayim.]

Abba Yahweh, the soul which You have given within me is pure. You have breathed it into me, and You preserve it within me. You will eventually take it from me, and restore it within me in Time to Come. So long as the soul is within me, I offer thanks to You, Yahweh my God, and God of my fathers. Master of all works, Lord of all souls, blessed is Yahweh who restores souls to dead bodies.

Blessed is Yahweh our God, King of the universe, who gives the rooster understanding to distinguish between day and night.

Blessed is Yahweh our God, King of the universe, who spreads forth the earth above the waters.

Blessed is Yahweh our God, King of the universe, who heals the sick, restores the body, opens the eyes of the blind, and directs the steps of man.

Blessed is Yahweh our God, King of the universe, who releases the prisoner. Blessed is He who liberates those who are in bondage.

Blessed is Yahweh our God, King of the universe, who grants favors to the unworthy and has granted me supreme favor by delivering me from my enemies.

Blessed is Yahweh our God, King of the universe, who straightens the bowed, and gives strength to the weary.

Blessed is Yahweh our God, King of the universe, who clothes the naked, and has provided me with my every need.

Blessed is Yahweh our God, King of the universe, who girds His people with might, and crowns His people with glory.

Blessed is Yahweh our God, King of the universe, who hears the cry of the afflicted, the orphan, the widow, and removes fear, anxiety and stress from our hearts.

Blessed is Yahweh our God, King of the universe, who has redeemed us by His Anointed One, Yahshua of Nazareth, son of David, Son of Yahweh.

Blessed is Yahweh our God, King of the universe, who removes sleep from my eyes and slumber from my eyelids.

May it be Your will Yahweh our God, and God of our fathers, to accustom us to study Your Scriptures, and to make us cleave to Your commandments. Do not bring us into sin, or into transgression or iniquity, or into temptation or scorn. And may the evil inclination not have mastery over us. Keep us far from an evil person and an evil companion, Make us cleave to good inclinations and good deeds, and compel our inclination to be subservient to You. Grant us this day and every day, grace, kindness and mercy in Your eyes and in the eyes of all who behold us. And bestow Your Holy Spirit and bountiful kindness upon your people.

May it be Your will Yahweh my God and God of my fathers, to protect me this day and every day from insolent men and from impudence. From a wicked man, from an evil neighbor, from an evil occurrence, from an evil eye, from a malicious tongue, from slander, from false testimony, from men's hate, from calumnious charges, from unnatural death, from harsh diseases and from misfortune, from the destructive adversary, from a harsh judgment, from an implacable opponent, whether or not he is a member of the Covenant, and from thc rctribution of thc gravc.

Blessed is Yahweh our God, King of the universe, who has sanctified us with Your commandments, and commanded us concerning the Words of Scripture. And make the teachings of Your Word, Yahweh our God, pleasant in our mouth and in the mouth of Your entire people, and may Your children all know Your Namc, and bc students of Your Scripture.

Blessed is Yahweh our God, King of universe, who has chosen us and given us You Holy Word. Blessed is Yahweh, who gives the TORAH.

Yahweh spoke to Moses, saying, "Speak to Aaron and to his sons, saying, thus shall you bless the children of Israel:"

> May Yahweh bless you and guard you. May Yahweh make His countenance shine upon you and be gracious to you. May Yahweh turn His countenance towards you and grant you peace.

[Y'varekh'kha Adonai v'yishm'rekha ya'er Adonai panau elekha vihuneka yisa Adonai panau elekha v'yasem L'kha Shalom.]

These are the precepts for which no fixed measure is prescribed. Leaving the crops of the edge of the field for the poor, the gift of the first fruits, the pilgrimage offerings brought when appearing before Yahweh on the Three Festivals, deeds of kindness, and study of Scripture. These are the precepts, the fruits of which man enjoys in this world, while the principal reward remains in the World to Come: Honoring one's father and mother, performing deeds of kindness, early attendance at the House of Study evening and morning, hospitality to strangers, visiting the sick, dowering the bride, escorting the dead, concentration in prayer, bringing peace between man and his fellowman and between husband and wife, and the study of the TORAH is equivalent to them all.

My soul, bless Yahweh! Yahweh my God, You are greatly exalted. You have garbed Yourself with majesty and splendor. You enwrap Yourself with light as with a garment. You spread the heavens as a curtain.

Blessed is Yahweh our God, King of the universe, who has sanctified us with His commandments, and commanded us to enwrap ourselves with a fringed garment.

How precious is Your kindness, O Yahweh! The children of men take refuge in the shadow of Your wings. They shall be satiated with the delight of Your House, and You will give them to drink from the river of Your pleasure. With You is the source of life. In Your Light we see light. Bestow Your Holy Spirit, Your kindness and Your righteousness on the upright of heart. Blessed is Yahweh our God, King of the universe, who has sanctified us with Your Commandments, and commanded us to meditate on Your TORAH.

SHACHARIT

~ Morning Prayer ~

How goodly are Your dwelling places Abba Father! I, through Your abundant kindness, come into Your house. I bow toward Your holy sanctuary in awe of You. May my prayer to You, Yahweh, be at a propitious time. In Your abounding kindness answer me with Your deliverance.

Lord of the universe, who reigned before anything was created-- at the time when by Your will all things were made, then was Your name proclaimed King. And after all things shall cease to be, the Awesome One will reign. You were, You are and You shall be in glory. You are one, and there is none to compare with You to consort with You without beginning, without end, power and dominion belong to You, You are my God and my everlasting Redeemer, the strength of my lot in time of distress. You are my banner and my refuge, my portion on the day I call, into Your hand I entrust my spirit, when I sleep and when I wake. And with my soul, my body too, Yahweh is with me, I shall not fear.

Yahweh our God and God of our fathers, remember us favorably before You, and be mindful of us for deliverance and mercy from the primeval, most supreme heavens. Remember in our behalf, Yahweh our God, the love of the Patriarchs, Abraham, Isaac and Jacob, Your servants, and the Covenant, the loving kindness, the vow which You have sworn to Abraham on Mount Moriah, and the 'Akedah', the binding of Isaac upon the altar, and the binding and sacrifice of Your Holy Anointed One, Yahshua.

A man should forever fear Yahweh in the inner-most recesses of his heart and acknowledge the Truth in his heart. Let him rise early and say:

> Abba Yahweh, Master of the world! It is not because of our own righteousness that we present our supplications before You, but because of Your abounding mercies, and the Sacrifice of Your Holy Anointed One, Yahshua, and His resurrection and ascension into heaven. What are we? What is our life? What is our kindness? What is our righteousness? What is our strength? What is

our might? What can we say to You, Yahweh our God and God of our fathers? Are not all the mighty men as nothing before You, men of renown as though they had never been, the wise as if without knowledge, and the men of understanding as if devoid of intelligence? For most of their deeds are naught, and the days of their lives are vanity before You. The preeminence of man over beast is naught, for all is vanity for all men must give an accounting before the Throne of Your Glory.

All nations are as nothing before You, as it is written. The nations are as a drop from a bucket, considered no more than dust upon the scales. But we are Your nation, the people of Your Covenant, the children of Abraham, Your beloved. The community of Yahshua, Your only begotten Son, whose name You called Immanuel, because of Your love for Him and Your delight in Him. And especially for the Sacrifice of Your Holy Anointed One Yahshua, who gave His life so that all men may come to know You the Mighty King and Master of the universe. Upon Him have You conferred the Messianic hope, the Messianic Covenant for all men who choose to believe in the testimony which You have given of Your only begotten Son Yahshua, son of David, and High Priest of Yahweh.

Therefore, it is incumbent upon us to thank, praise and glorify You, to bless, to sanctify and to offer praise and thanksgiving to Your Name. How good is our portion, how pleasant our lot, and how beautiful our heritage! Fortunate are we who, in the evening and early in the morning, twice each day, declare:

> Hear, O Israel, Yahweh is our God, Yahweh is One. Blessed is His Name, and His glorious Kingdom forever and ever.

> [Shema yisra-ayl Adonai eloheinu Adonai echad. Baruch shem k'vod mal'chuso l'olam va-ed]

You shall love Yahweh your God with all your heart, with all your soul, and with all your might. And these words which I command you today shall be upon your heart. You shall teach them diligently to your children, and you shall speak of them when you walk on the road, when you lie down and when you rise. You shall bind them as a sign upon your hand, and they shall be as frontlets between your eyes, and you shall write them upon the doorposts of your house and upon your gates.

[V'ahavta ays Adonai elohecha, b'chal l'vav'cha, u-v'chal naf-sh'cha, u-l'chal m'odecha. V'ha-yu ha-d'varim ha-ayleh asher anochi m'tzav'cha ha-yom al l'va-vecha. V'shinan-tam l'vanecha v'dibarta bam, b'shiv-t'cha b'vay secha, u-v'lech-t'cha vaderech, u-v'shach-b'cha, u-v'kumecha. U-k'shartam l'os al yadecha, v'ha-yu l'totafos bayn aynecha. U-ch'savtam al m'zuzos bay-secha, u-vish'arecha.]

And it will be, if you will diligently keep My commandments to love Yahweh your God and to serve Him with all your heart and with all your soul, I will give rain for your land at the proper time, the early rain and the latter rain, and you will gather in your grain, your wine and your oil. And I will give grass in your fields for your cattle, and you will eat and be sated.

Take care less your heart be lured away, and you turn astray and worship alien gods and bow down to them. For then Yahweh's wrath will flare up against you, and He will close the heavens so that there will be no rain and the earth will not yield its produce, and you will swiftly perish from the good land which Yahweh gives you.

Therefore, place these words of Mine upon your heart and upon your soul, and bind them for a sign on your hand, and they shall he as frontlets [reminders] between your eyes. You shall teach them to your children, to speak of them when you sit in your house and when you walk on the road, when you lie down and when you rise. You shall inscribe them on the doorposts of your house and on your gates--so that your days and the days of your children may be prolonged on the land which Yahweh swore to your fathers to give them for as long as the heavens are above the earth.

Yahweh spoke to Moses, saying. Speak to the children of Israel and tell them to make for themselves fringes on the corners of their garments throughout their generations, and to attach a thread of blue on the fringe of each corner. They shall be to you as tzitzit, and you shall look upon them and remember all the commandments of Yahweh and fulfill them, and you will not follow after your heart and after your eyes by which you go astray-- so that you may remember and fulfill all My commandments and be holy to your God. I am Yahweh your God who brought you out of the land of Egypt to be your God. I, Yahweh, am your God.

You were the same before the world was created. You are the same since the world has been created. You are the same in this world. You are the same in the World to Come. Sanctify Your Name in Your world upon those who hallow Your Name. Through Your salvation, our King, raise and exalt our strength, and deliver us speedily for the sake of Your Name, for the sake of Your Word, and for the sake of the Sacrifice upon the tree of Your Son Yahshua.

You are Yahweh the Most High God in heaven and on earth, and in the most lofty heaven of heavens. Truly, You are the First and You are the Last, and besides You there is no god. Gather the dispersed who long for You from the four corners of the earth. Let all mankind recognize and know that You alone are God over all the kingdoms of the earth. You have made the heavens, the earth, the sea, and all that is therein. Who among all the works of Your hands, celestial or terrestrial, can say to You: What are You doing? What are You making?

Our living and eternal Father in heaven, deal graciously and kindly with us for the sake of Your great, mighty and awe-inspiring Name which is conferred upon us. Fulfill for us, Yahweh our God, the promise which You have made to us through Zephaniah Your prophet, as it is written: At that time, I will bring you back, and at that time I will gather you. For I will make you renowned and glorified among all the peoples of the earth when I bring back your captivity before your eyes, saith Yahweh.

May it be Your will, Yahweh our God and God of our fathers to have mercy on us and forgive all our sins, and accept the atonement of Yahshua, the Holy Anointed One of Yahweh to forgive all our iniquities and to forgive and pardon all our transgressions. May Yahweh, in His great mercy return upon His children the promise of the coming of His Holy Anointed One Yahshua, to set up His Kingdom here on earth, and may it be that we, and all those who worship and bow down to Your most Holy Name, grant that we too may sit and reign with Him in His Kingdom, as promised in Your Scriptures for the Messianic Covenant.

Abba Father, we implore You, in the name of Yahshua, release us from bondage. Accept our Prayers, strengthen us, purify us Awesome One, Mighty One, we beseech You, guard as the apple of Your eye those who seek Your Salvation. Bless us, cleanse us, bestow upon us forever Your merciful righteousness.

Powerful, Holy One, in Your abounding goodness, guide us. Only and Exalted One, turn to those who are mindful of Your holiness, accept our supplications, hear our cry and answer us speedily in the day that we call.

Blessed be Your Name and your glorious Kingdom forever and ever.

[Baruch shem k'vod mal'chuso l'olam va-ed.]

MINCHAH

~ Afternoon Prayer ~

Blessed is Yahweh our God-King of the Universe. Happy are those who dwell in Your House. We will yet praise You forever. Happy are those whose lot is thus. Happy are those whose God is Yahweh.

I will exalt You, my God and Bless Your Name forever. Everyday I will bless You, and extol Your Name forever. Yahweh is great and exceedingly exalted, there is no limit to Your greatness. One generation to another will laud Your works, and tell of Your mighty acts.

I will speak of the splendor of Your glorious majesty and of Your wondrous deeds. I will speak of Your mercy and sing of Your righteousness.

Yahweh is gracious and compassionate, slow to anger and of great kindness. Yahweh is good to all, and His mercies extend over all His works. The righteous will make known to men His mighty acts, and the glorious majesty of His Kingdom. Your Kingship is a Kingship over all nations, and Your dominion throughout all generations. Yahweh supports all who fall, and lifts up all who bow down. The eyes of all look expectantly to You, and You give them their food at the proper time. You open Your hand and satisfy the desire of every living thing. Yahweh is righteous in all His ways, and benevolent in all His deeds.

Yahweh is close to all who call upon Him, to all who call upon Him in truth. He fulfills the desire of those who fear Him. He hears their cry and delivers them. Yahweh watches over all who love Him, and will destroy all the wicked. My mouth will praise Yahweh, and let all flesh Bless His Holy Name forever. We will Bless Yahweh from now and forever. Praise be to Yahweh.

MAARIV

~ Evening Prayer ~

Blessed is Yahweh our God-King of the Universe. Who by His Word causes the evenings to become dark. With wisdom He opens the gates, with understanding He changes the periods, varies the times, and arranges the stars in their positions in the sky according to His will. He creates day and night; He rolls away light before darkness and darkness before light. He causes day to pass and brings on the night, and separates between day and night. Yahweh of hosts is His Name. Blessed is Yahweh, who causes the evenings to become dark.

With an everlasting love You have loved Your people. You have taught us Scripture, decrees, and laws. Therefore, Yahweh our God, when we lie down and when we rise, we will speak of Your statutes and rejoice in the Words of Your TORAH forever. For they are our life and the length of our days, and we will meditate on them day and night. May Your love never depart from us.

Blessed is Yahweh, who loves His people.

Truth and belief is all this, it is established that He is Yahweh our God. There is no other, and that we are His people and the sheep of His pasture. It is He who redeems us from the hand of our enemies. Our King delivers us from the grip of tyrants. The benevolent God avenges us against our persecutors, and brings retribution on all our mortal enemies. He does great things beyond limit, and wonders beyond number. He has kept us alive, and did not allow our feet to falter. He led us upon the high places of our foes, and increased our strength over all our adversaries. He is a benevolent God who brings retribution upon our enemies and has brought us out from their midst to an everlasting freedom. Yahweh has brought forth His Holy Anointed One, Yahshua, son of David and High Priest of Yahweh to deliver us from the paths of sin into a land of milk and honey, a land of peace and everlasting joy.

Indeed, the righteous will extol the Name of Yahshua, the upright will dwell in Your presence forever. Therefore we hope that You may soon come to reign over us. That all mankind shall invoke the Name of Yahshua, to turn to You all the wicked of the world. Then all the inhabitants of the world will recognize and know that at the Name of

Yahshua, every knee shall bend, and every tongue shall confess that Yahshua is Lord.

Before You Yahweh our God, they will bow and prostrate themselves, and give honor and glory to Your Name, and they will all take upon themselves the yoke of Your Kingdom. And for all eternity You shall reign in glory, and as it is written in the TORAH: Yahweh shall be King over the entire earth, on that day Yahweh shall be One and His Name One. Blessed is Yahweh who has pleaded our cause, has delivered us from bondage and from the hand of our enemies, and has caused their wickedness to return upon their own heads.

May Yahweh grant all the desires of our hearts, fulfill all our purposes and all our petitions. May Yahweh hear from heaven, answer quickly all our requests and save us in the day of trouble. In the Name of Yahshua defend us and send from heaven help to deliver us from bondage, from our enemies and from poverty. In Yahshua' Name we pray-Amen.

Prayer Before

~ Retiring at Night ~

Master of the universe, I hereby forgive anyone who has angered or vexed me, or sinned against me, either physically or financially, against my honor or anything else that is mine, whether by speech, or by deeds. May no man be punished on my account. May it be Your will, Yahweh my God and God of my fathers, that I shall sin no more, nor repeat my sins, neither shall I again anger You nor do what is wrong in Your eyes. The sins I have committed, erase in Your abounding mercies, but not through suffering of severe illness, but by the shed Blood of Yahshua the Messiah. May the words of my mouth and the meditation of my heart by acceptable before You, Yahweh my strength and my Redeemer.

Our Father, let us lie down in peace. Our King, raise us up to a good life and peace, improve us with Your good counsel, help us speedily for the sake of Your name, and spread over us the shelter of Your peace. Protect us and remove from us the enemy, pestilence, sword, famine, and sorrow. Remove the adversary from before us and from behind us. Shelter us in the shadow of Your wings, and guard our going out and our coming in for a good life and peace from now and forever. For You, Yahweh are a benevolent God, You are our guardian and our deliver.

> Hear, O Israel, Yahweh is our God, Yahweh is One. Blessed is His Name, and His glorious Kingdom forever and ever.

> [Shema yisra-ayl Adonai eloheinu Adonai echad. Baruch shem k'vod mal'chuso l'olam va-ed]

You shall love Yahweh your God with all your heart, with all your soul, and with all your might. And these words which I command you today shall be upon your heart. You shall teach them diligently to your children, and you shall speak of them when you sit in your house and when you walk on the road, when you lie down and when you rise. You shall bind them as a sign upon your hand, and they shall be as frontlets between your eyes. And you shall write them upon the doorposts of your house and upon your gates.

And it shall be, if you will diligently keep all My commandments to love Yahweh your God and to serve Him with all your heart and with all your soul, I will give rain for your land at the proper time, the early rain and the latter rain, and you will gather in your grain, your wine, and your oil. And I will give grass in your fields for your cattle, and you will eat and be sated.

Take care lest your heart be lured away, and you turn astray and worship alien gods and bow down to them. For then Yahweh's wrath will flare up against you, and He will close the heavens so that there will be no rain and the earth will not yield its produce, and you will swiftly perish from the good land which Yahweh gives you. Therefore, place these words of Mine upon your heart and upon your soul, and bind them for a sign on your hand, and they shall be as frontlets before your eyes.

You shall teach them to your children, to speak of them when you sit in your house, when you walk on the road, when you lie down and when you rise up. You shall bind them as a sign upon your hand, and they shall be as frontlets between your eyes, and you shall inscribe them on the doorposts of your house and on your gates-so that your days and the days of your children may be prolonged on the land which Yahwch sworc to your fathers to give them for as long as the heavens are above the earth.

Blessed is Yahweh our God, King of the Universe, who has sanctified us with His commandments, and commanded us concerning the washing of the hands.

[Baruch atah Adonai eloheinu, melech ha-Olam. Asher kid'shanu b'mitzvotav v'tzivanu al n'tilas yadayim.]

May Yahweh bless you and keep you. May Yahweh make His countenance shine upon you and be gracious to you. May Yahweh turn His countenance towards you and grant you peace.

[Y'varekh'kha Adonai v'yishm'rekha ya'er Adonai panau elekha vihuneka yisa Adonai panau elekha v'yasem l'kha Shalom.]

He who dwells in the shelter of the Most High, who abides in the shadow of the Almighty, I say of Yahweh, who is my refuge and my stronghold, my God in whom I trust, that Yahweh will save me from the ensnaring trap, from the destructive pestilence. He will cover me with His pinions and I will find refuge under His wings, His truth is a shield and an armor. I shall not fear the terror of the night, nor the arrow that flies by day, the pestilence that prowls in the darkness, nor the destruction that ravages at noon. A thousand may fall at my side, and ten thousand at my right hand, but it shall not touch me. I need only look with my eyes, and I will see the retribution of the wicked. Because I have said, Yahshua is my shelter, and I have made the Most High my haven

Our God and God of my fathers, may our prayers come before You, and do not turn away from our supplications. You know the mysteries of the universe and the hidden secrets of every living soul. You search out all our innermost thoughts, and probe our minds and hearts. Nothing is hidden from You, nothing is concealed from Your sight. And so, may it be Your will Yahweh our God and God of our fathers, to have mercy on us and forgive us all our sins, and grant us atonement through the shed Blood of Your Holy Anointed One, Yahshua, to forgive all our iniquities and to forgive and pardon us for all our transgressions.

Abba Father, we implore You, in the Name of Yahshua, to release us from bondage. Accept our prayers, strengthen us, and purify us Awesome One, the Mighty One, we beseech You, guard as the apple of Your eye those who seek Your salvation. Bless us, cleanse us, bestow upon us forever Your merciful righteousness. Powerful, Holy One, in Your abounding goodness, guide Your people. Only and Exalted One, turn to those who are mindful of Your holiness. Accept our supplication and hear our cry.

Blessed is Your Name and Your glorious Kingdom forever and ever.

[Baruch shem k'vod mal'chuso l'olam va-ed.]

Be gracious to me, Abba Yahweh, in keeping with Your kindness. In accordance with Your abounding compassion erase my transgressions. Cleanse me thoroughly of my wrongdoing, and purify me of my sin. I acknowledge my transgressions, and my sin is always before me. Against You alone have I sinned and done that which is evil in Your eyes. Forgive me, in the Name of Yahshua so that You will be justified in Your verdict, and vindicated in Your judgment.

Purge me with hyssop and I shall be pure. Cleanse me and I shall be whiter than snow. Let me hear joy and gladness. Hide Your face from my sins, and erase all my trespasses. Create in me a clean heart Abba Yahweh, and renew within me an upright spirit. Do not cast me out of Your presence and do not take Your Holy Spirit from me. Restore to me the joy of Your deliverance, and uphold me with a spirit of mercy. Save me from bloodguilt, Abba Yahweh and my tongue will sing Your righteousness.

Abba Yahweh open my lips and my mouth shall declare Your praise. For You do not desire sacrifice, nor do You wish burnt offerings. The sacrifice of Yahweh is a contrite spirit, a contrite and broken heart. In Your good will help us rebuild the walls of Jerusalem.

I will lift up mine eyes unto the hills, from whence cometh my help. My help comes from Yahweh, who made heaven and earth. He will not suffer my foot to be moved, He that keeps me will not slumber. Behold, He that keeps Israel shall neither slumber nor sleep. Yahweh is my keeper. He is my shade upon my right hand. The sun shall not smite me by day or the moon by night. Yahweh shall preserve me from all evil. He shall preserve my soul. Yahweh shall preserve my going out and my coming in from this time forth, and forevermore.

When I lie down, I will not be afraid. I will lie down, and my sleep will be sweet. May I sleep well, may I awake in mercy. For Your salvation and in Your Holy Word I hope Yahweh. You are a refuge for me, protect me from disasters, and surround me with songs of deliverance forever. Make known to me the path of life that I may be satiated with the joy of Your presence and with the bliss of Your right hand forever.

Arise and have mercy on Zion, for it is time to be gracious to her. The appointed time has come. Thus shall You say to them: The god's that have not made the heavens and the earth shall perish from the earth and from under these heavens. I entrust my spirit into Your hands. You will redeem me Yahweh, God of truth.

Blessed is Yahweh our God, King of the universe, who causes the bonds of sleep to fall upon my eyes and slumber upon my eyelids, and who gives light to the apple of the eye. May it be Your will, Yahweh my God and God of my fathers, to let me lie down in peace and raise me up to a good life and peace. Let my thoughts not trouble me, or bad dreams, or sinful fancies, and may by bed be perfect before You. Give light to my eyes lest I sleep the sleep of death. Blessed is Yahweh, who in His glory gives light to the whole world.

Abba Father, who is in heaven, hallowed be Your Name. Your Kingdom come, Your will be done on earth as it is in heaven. Give us this day our daily bread, and forgive us our debts, as we forgive our debtors. Lead us not into temptation, but deliver us from evil. For Your's is the Kingdom, the Power, and the Glory forever and ever. Amen.

We cried out to Yahweh in our distress, Yahweh saved us from our afflictions. We cried out to Yahweh in our distress, and Yahweh brought us out of our calamity. Yahweh raises the needy from distress, and makes our families as numerous as flocks. The upright observe this and rejoice.

In the Name of Yahshua, I call upon the power of Yahweh to protect, encourage and strengthen the intimate bond of love between myself and my beloved. May Yahweh grant all the desires of our hearts, fulfill all our purposes, and all our petitions.

May Yahweh hear from heaven, answer quickly all our requests and save us in the day of trouble. In the Name of Yahshua defend us and send help from heaven to deliver us from bondage, from our enemies, and from poverty. In the Name of Yahshua we pray [B'shem Yahshua HaMashiach] Amen and Amen.

AMIDAH

Shemoneh Esreh

~ Silent Prayer ~

Silent Prayer said Standing while facing east

Abba Father open my lips, and my mouth shall declare Your praise. Blessed is Yahweh our God and God of our fathers, God of Abraham, God of Isaac, and God of Jacob. The great mighty and awesome God, exalted God, who bestows bountiful kindness, who creates all things, who remembers the piety of the Patriarchs, and who in love, has brought Yahshua our Redeemer to us, for the sake of Your Holy Name.

O King You are a helper, a savior and a shield. Blessed is Yahweh, shield of Abraham. You are mighty forever, Abba Father. You are powerful to save. You cause the dew to descend, the wind to blow, and the rain to fall. You sustain the living with loving kindness, resurrect the dead with great mercy, support the falling, heal the sick, release those in bondage, and fulfill Your trust to those who sleep in the dust. Who is like You, Mighty One! And who can be compared to You our King, who brings death and restores life, and causes deliverance to spring forth! Who is like You merciful Father, who in compassion remembers Your creatures for life. You are trustworthy to revive the dead. Blessed is Yahweh, who revives the dead.

You are holy and Your Name is holy, and the Holy Angels praise You daily for all eternity. Blessed is Yahweh, the Holy God. You graciously bestow wisdom, understanding and knowledge upon us. Blessed is Yahweh, who graciously bestows His knowledge upon us.

Cause us to return, our Father, to Your written TORAH. Draw us near our King to Your service, and bring us back to You in whole-hearted repentance. Blessed is Yahweh who desires repentance.

Pardon us, our Father, for we have sinned. Forgive us, our King, for we have transgressed. You are a good and forgiving God. Blessed is Yahweh, the gracious One, who pardons abundantly.

Behold our affliction and wage our battles. Redeem us speedily for the sake of Your Name, for the sake of Your Word, and for the sake of Yahshua, the Anointed One, our Savior and our Redeemer. Blessed is Yahweh, Redeemer of lost souls. Heal us Abba Father, and we will be healed. Help us and we will be saved, for you are our praise. Grant complete cure and healing to all our wounds. For You are a faithful and merciful healer, as it is written in Your Scriptures: By His stripes we are healed. And again in the Messianic Covenant: by His stripes we were healed. Blessed is Yahweh who heals the sick of His people in the Name of His Holy Anointed One, Yahshua, we pray.

Bless for us, Yahweh our God, this year and all the varieties of its produce for good. And bestow blessings upon the face of the earth. Satisfy us from Your bounty and bless our year like other good years for blessing. For You are a generous God who bestows goodness and blesses the years. Make known to me the path of life that I may be satiated with the joy of Your presence and with the bliss of Your right hand forever. Sound the trumpet for our freedom, raise a banner to gather the dispersed and bring us together from the four corners of the earth. Blessed is Yahweh, who gathers the dispersed of His people. Remove from us sorrow and sighing, and reign over us, with kindness and compassion, with righteousness and justice. ,

Blessed is Yahweh, our faithful King, who loves righteousness and justice. Let there be no hope for informers, or heretics and may all the wicked instantly perish. May all our enemies be speedily extirpated, and may You swiftly uproot, break, crush and subdue the reign of wickedness speedily in our days. Blessed is Yahweh, who crushes our enemies and subdues the wicked.

May Your mercies be aroused Yahweh our God, upon us. Grant ample reward to all who truly trust in Your Name, and place our lot among the righteous. May we never be disgraced, for we have put our trust in You. Blessed is Yahweh who is the support and salvation of the righteous.

Return in mercy to Jerusalem and dwell therein as You have promised. Speedily establish therein the throne of David Your servant, and rebuild the walls in our days as an everlasting edifice. Blessed is Yahweh who rebuilds the walls of Jerusalem.

Speedily cause the son of David, Yahshua of Nazareth, to flourish, and increase His power by Your salvation, for we hope for Your salvation, as it is written in Your Scriptures for the Messianic Covenant that it is in His Name that we are saved from our sins. Blessed is Yahweh, who causes the power of His salvation to flourish.

Hear our voice, Yahweh our God, Merciful Father, have compassion upon us and accept our prayers in mercy and favor, for You are a God who hears our prayers and supplications. Do not turn us away empty-handed from You our King, for You hear our prayers. Blessed is Yahweh, who hears our prayer. Look with favor, Yahweh our God, on Your people, and pay heed to our prayer. Rebuild the walls of Jerusalem, raise up the Tabernacle of David in our days, and accept with love and favor our praise offerings and prayers. May the service of Your people always find favor in Your eyes.

May our eyes behold Your return to Zion in Mercy. Blessed is Yahweh, who restores Your Divine Presence in Zion. Bestow peace, goodness and blessing, life, graciousness, kindness and mercy upon us and upon all Your people. Bless us, our Father with the light of Your countenance. You gave us, Yahweh our God, the TORAH of life and loving-kindness, righteousness, blessing, mercy, life and peace. May it be favorable in Your eyes to bless Your people at all times and at every moment with Your peace. Blessed is Yahweh, who blesses His people with peace.

Abba Father guard my tongue from evil and my lips from speaking deceitfully. Let my soul be silent to those who curse me. Let my soul be as dust to all. Open my heart to Your TORAH, and let my soul eagerly pursue Your commandments. As for all those who plot evil against me, hasten to annul their counsel and frustrate their design. Let them be as chaff before the wind. Let the Angels of Yahweh thrust them away. That Your beloved ones may be delivered, help with Your right hand and answer me. Do it for the sake of Your Name, do it for the sake of Your right hand, do it for the sake of Your Holy Anointed One, Yahshua the Messiah, do it for the sake of Your Holiness. May the words of my mouth and the meditation of my heart be acceptable before You Yahweh my Strength and my Redeemer.

He who makes peace in His heavens may He make peace for us and for all His people, and say, Amen. May it be Your will, Yahweh our God and God of our Fathers, that the walls of Jerusalem, and the Temple be rebuilt in our days, and grant us a portion in the Lamb's Book of Life. May there be abundant peace from heaven, and a good life for us and for all Israel. Amen and Amen.

READING OF THE SCRIPTURES

This is the written TORAH which Moses placed before the children of Israel. It is a tree of life for those who hold fast to it, and those who support it are fortunate. Its ways are pleasant ways and all its paths are peace, long life is at its right, riches and honor are at its left. Yahweh has desired, for the sake of His righteousness, to make His Word great and glorious.

May Yahweh help, shield and deliver all who trust in Him, and let us say, Amen. Let us all render glory to Yahweh and give honor to His TORAH. Blessed is He who in His holiness gave the TORAH to His people.

Blessed is Yahweh who is blessed for all eternity. Blessed is Yahweh our God, King of the universe, who had chosen us from among all the peoples of the world and has given us His Holy Word.

Blessed is Yahweh our God, King of the universe, who has chosen good prophets and found favor with their words, which were spoken in truth. Blessed is Yahweh, who has chosen the Scriptures, Moses Your servant, the prophets of truth and righteousness, Yahshua Your Anointed One, and we the sheep of Your pasture.

Blessed is Yahweh our God, King of the universe, creator of the world, righteous in all generations, faithful God, who says and does, who speaks and fulfills, for all Your words are true and just. You are trustworthy. Not one of Your words returns unfulfilled. For You, Almighty King, are trustworthy and compassionate. Blessed is Yahweh, the God who is trustworthy in all Your words. Bring deliverance and joy to the humiliated spirit speedily in our days. Blessed is Yahweh our God who causes Zion to rejoice in her children.

SABBATH WELCOME

To light the Sabbath Candles:

> Blessed is Yahweh our God, King of universe, who has sanctified us with His commandments, and commanded us to kindle the light of the Holy Sabbath.

> [Baruch atah Adonai eloheinu, melech ha-olam asher kid'shanu b'mitzvotav v'tzivanu l'hadlik ner shel Shabbat kodesh.]

And the children of Israel shall observe the Sabbath, establishing the Sabbath throughout their generations as an everlasting covenant. It is a sign between Yahweh and the children of Israel for all time, for in six days Yahweh made the heavens and the earth, and on the seventh day He ceased from work and rested.

If you restrain your feet because of the Sabbath from attending to your affairs on Yahweh's holy day, and you call the Sabbath a delight, the day made holy by Yahweh, honored, and you honor it by not following your customary ways, refraining from pursuing your affairs and speaking profane things, then you shall delight in Yahweh, and He will make you ride on the high places of the earth. And He will nourish you with the heritage of Yahshua your Savior.

This is the meal of the holy ancient One. Remember the Sabbath to sanctify it. Six days you shall labor and do all your work, but the seventh day is the Sabbath for Yahweh your God. You shall not do any work-you, your son or your daughter, your manservant or your maidservant, or your cattle, or the stranger within your gates. For in six days Yahweh made the heavens, the earth, the sea, and all that is in them, and rested on the seventh day. Therefore Yahweh blessed the Sabbath and made it holy.

Hear, O Israel, Yahweh is our God, Yahweh is One. Blessed is His Name, and His glorious Kingdom forever and ever.

[Shema yisra-ayl Adonai eloheinu Adonai echad. Baruch shem k'vod mal'chuso l'olam va-ed.]

You shall love Yahweh your God with all your heart, with all your soul, and with all your might. And these words which I command you today shall be upon your heart. You shall teach them diligently to your children, and you shall speak of them when you sit in your house and when you walk on the road, when you lie down and when you rise. You shall bind them as a sign upon your hand, and they shall be as reminders between your eyes. And you shall write them upon the doorposts of your house and upon your gates.

And it will be, if you will diligently obey my commandments to love Yahweh your God and to serve Him with all your heart and with all your soul, I will give rain for your land at the proper time. The early rain and the latter rain, and you will gather in your grain, your wine and your oil. And I will give grass in your fields for your cattle. And you will eat and be sated.

Take care lest your heart be lured away, and you turn astray and worship alien gods and bow down to them. For then Yahweh's wrath will flare up against you, and He will close the heavens so that there will be no rain and the earth will not yield its produce, and you will swiftly perish from the good land which Yahweh gives you.

Open my lips Father and my mouth shall declare Your praise. Blessed is Yahweh our God and God of our fathers, the great, mighty and awesome God who bestows bountiful kindness, and faithfulness, who creates all things, who remembers the piety of Your Holy Ones, and who, in love, has brought the Redeemer, and placed Your Holy Spirit upon us for the sake of His holy Name. Heal us, Father, and we will be healed. Help us and we will be saved, for You are our praise. Grant complete cure and healing to all our wounds. Blessed is Yahweh who heals the sick of His people.

THE HUSBAND
~ BLESSES THE WIFE ~

Blessed is Yahweh our God, King of the universe and bless my beloved, for who can find a virtuous woman? Her price is far above rubies. The heart of her husband safely trusts in her, so that he shall have no need of spoil. She will do me good and not evil all the days of her life. Strength and honor are her clothing, and she shall rejoice in time to come. She opens her mouth with wisdom, and in her tongue is the law of kindness. She looks well to the ways of her household, and eats not the bread of idleness.

Her children rise up and call her blessed, her husband also, and he praises her, "Many daughters have done virtuously, but you excel them all. I ask Yahweh, in the Name of Yahshua the Messiah, to abundantly bless you in your life and in everything you do. I ask Yahweh, to abundantly bless you with good health and prosperity all the days of your life." Favor is deceitful, and beauty is vain, but a woman that fears Yahweh shall be praised. Give her of the fruit of her hands, and let her own works praise her.

I pray for my beloved Father, I pray for her spirit, her traveling mercies, her health, her relationships, her priorities, her fears, her protection, her desires and her future. I call upon the power of Yahweh to protect and encourage the intimate bond of love between my beloved and I.

THE WIFE
~ BLESSES THE HUSBAND ~

Blessed is the man that fears the Lord that delights greatly in His commandments. His seed shall be mighty upon the earth and the generations of the upright shall be blessed. Wealth and riches shall be in his house, and his righteousness endures forever.

A good man shows favor, he is gracious, and full of compassion and righteousness. He will guide his affairs with discretion. His heart is established, he shall not be afraid of evil tidings, he is always trusting in the Lord. He shall see his desire upon his enemies.

He has dispersed, he has given to the poor; his horn shall be exalted with honor. The wicked shall see it and be grieved; he shall gnash with his teeth and melt away. The desire of the wicked shall perish. But the righteous man shall endure forever and ever. Praise the Lord.

May Yahweh hear you in the day of trouble and may the God of Jacob defend you against all your enemies, send help from the sanctuary, and strengthen you out of Zion. May Yahweh remember all your offerings, grant you according to your heart's desire and fulfill all your counsel. We will rejoice in your salvation and in the Name of Yahweh our God we will set up our banners.

I know that Yahweh saves His anointed. Yahweh will hear from His holy heaven with the saving strength of His right hand. Some trust in chariots, and some in horses, but we will remember the Name of Yahweh our God. Praise the Lord.

~ THE BLESSING OF THE CHILDEN ~

May Yahweh, God of our fathers, make you a thousand times more numerous than you are, and bless you as He promised you. Blessed shall you be in the city, and blessed shall you be in the field. Blessed shall be your basket and your kneading bowl. Blessed shall be the fruit of your land, the fruit of your livestock, the increase of your cattle and the offspring of your sheep. Blessed shall you be in your coming, and blessed shall you be in your going. Yahweh will command the blessing to be with you in your storehouses and in all things to which you put your hand, and He will bless you in the land which Yahweh your God gives to you.

Yahweh will open for you His good treasure the heavens to give rain for your land at its proper time, and to bless all the works of your hands. You will lend too many nations but you will not borrow. For Yahweh your God has blessed you as He has promised you. Fortunate are the children of Yahweh!

The children of Yahweh will be delivered by Yahweh with an everlasting deliverance. You will not be disgraced or humiliated forever and ever. You will eat and be satiated and praise the Name of Yahweh your God who has dealt with you wondrously, and My people will never be put to shame. And you will know that I am within My people that I am Yahweh your God, and there is none else.

KIDDUSH

A Psalm of David, Yahweh is our Shepherd. We shall not want. Yahweh makes us to lie down in green pastures. He leads us beside the still waters. He restores our souls. Yahweh leads us in the paths of righteousness for His name's sake. Yea, though we walk through the valley of the shadow of death, we will fear no evil, for Yahweh is with us. Thy rod and Thy staff they comfort us. Yahweh prepares a table before us in the presence of our enemies. Yahweh anoints our heads with oil, our cups runneth over. Surely goodness and mercy shall follow us all the days of our lives, and we shall dwell in the House of Yahweh forever.

In the Scripture it is written that Yahshua declared, I am the good Shepherd, and I know My sheep, and I am known of Mine. I am the door of the sheep. I am the door, by Me if any man enters in, he shall be saved, and shall go in and out, and find pasture. I am the good Shepherd the good Shepherd gives His life for the sheep. As the Father knows Me, even so know I the Father, and I lay down My life for the sheep. And other sheep I have, which are not of this fold, them also I must bring, and they shall hear My voice, and there shall be one fold, and one Shepherd.

Therefore does My Father love Me, because I lay down My life, that I might take it again No man takes it from Me, but I lay it down, and I have power to take it up again. This commandment have I received of My Father.

Prepare the meal of perfect faith, which is the delight of the holy King. Prepare the meal of the King. This is the meal of the holy divine presence of His Anointed One Yahshua the Messiah, and the holy Ancient One comes to join in the meal.

On the same night in which He was betrayed, Yahshua rose up from supper, laid aside His garments, and took a towel and girded Himself. After that He poured water into a basin, and began to wash the Disciples feet, and to wipe them with the towel wherewith He was girded. So after He had washed their feet, and taken His garments and was set down again, He said unto them, "If I then, Lord and Master, have washed your feet, you also ought to wash one another's feet."

Blessed is Yahweh our God, King of the universe, who has sanctified us with His commandments, and commanded us concerning the washing of the hands.

[Baruch atah Adonai eloheinu, melech ha-Olam Asher kid'shanu b'mitzvotav v'tzivanu al n'tilas yadayim.]

Likewise, Yahshua took bread and when He had given thanks, He broke it and said: "Take, eat. This is My body, which is broken for you, do this in remembrance of Me."

Blessed is Yahweh our God, King of the universe, who brings forth bread from the earth.

[Baruch atah Adonai eloheinu, melech ha-olam ha-motsea l'kim min ha-aretz]

And, in the same manner also He took the cup, saying: "This cup is the New Testament in My blood, do this as often as you drink it, in remembrance of me. For as often as you eat this bread, and drink this cup, you show Yahshua's death till He come." So likewise do we bless the wine, saying:

Blessed is Yahweh our God, King of the Universe, who creates the fruit of the wine.

[Baruch atah Adonai eloheinu, melech ha-olam borei prei ha-gafen.]

Blessed is Yahweh our God, King of the universe, who has sanctified us with His commandments, has desired us, and has given us, in love and good will, His holy Sabbath as a heritage in remembrance of the work of creation, the first of the holy festivals. For He has chosen us and sanctified us from among all the peoples, and with love and good will given us His holy Sabbath.

THE FAMILY PRAYS TOGETHER

May Yahweh grant all the desires of our hearts, fulfill all our purposes and all our petitions. May Yahweh hear from heaven, quickly answer all our requests and save us in the day of adversity. In the Name of Yahshua the Messiah defend us from our enemies, from poverty, and from bondage.

Everyone Says:

SABBATH SHALOM

BLESSINGS FOR THE SABBATH

To light the Sabbath Candles:

> Blessed is Yahweh our God, King of universe, who has sanctified us with His commandments, and commanded us to kindle the light of the Holy Sabbath.
>
> [Baruch atah Adonai eloheinu, melech ha-olam asher kid'shanu b'mitzvotav v'tzivanu l'hadlik ner shel Shabbat kodesh.]

A Psalm of David. Render to Yahweh, children of the mighty, render to Yahweh honor and strength. Render to Yahweh the honor due to His Name. Bow down to Yahweh in resplendent holiness. The voice of Yahweh is over waters, the God of glory thunders, Yahweh is over mighty waters. The voice of Yahweh resounds with might. The voice of Yahweh breaks cedars. Yahweh shatters the cedars of Lebanon. He makes them leap like a calf. Lebanon and Sirion like a young wild ox. The voice of Yahweh strikes flames of fire. The voice of Yahweh causes the desert of Kadesh to tremble. The voice of Yahweh causes the does to calve, and strips the forests bare, and in His sanctuary all proclaim His glory. Yahweh sat as King at the Flood. Yahweh will sit as King forever. Yahweh will give strength to His people. Yahweh will bless His people with peace.

Abba Father, we implore You, in the Name of Yahshua, and by the power of Your right hand, release us from bondage. Accept our prayers, strengthen us, purify us Awesome One, Mighty One, we beseech You, guard as the apple of Your eye those who seek Your Salvation. Bless us, cleanse us bestow upon us forever Your merciful righteousness. Powerful, Holy One, in Your abounding goodness guide us. Only and Exalted One, turn to those who are mindful of Your holiness. Accept our supplication and hear our cry.

Blessed is Your Name and Your glorious Kingdom forever and ever.

[Baruch shem k'vod mal'chuso l'olam va-ed.]

Come, my Beloved, to meet the Bride. Let us welcome the Sabbath. Observe and remember the one and only God caused us to hear in a single utterance, Yahweh is One and His Name is One, for renown, for glory and for praise.

Come let us welcome the Sabbath, for it is the source of blessing, from the beginning, from aforetime, it was chosen, last in creation, first in Yahweh's thought. Sanctuaries of the King, the royal city, arise, go forth from the ruins. Too long have you dwelt in the veil of tears, Yahweh will show you abounding mercy. Shake off the dust, arise, put on your glorious garments my people, through Yahshua, the son of David, draw near to my soul and redeem it.

Do not be ashamed or confounded. Why are you downcast and why are you agitated? The afflicted of my people will find refuge in you the city will be rebuilt on its former site. Those who despoil you will be despoiled, and all who would destroy you will be far away. Your God will rejoice over you as a bridegroom rejoices over his bride.

To the right and to the left you shall spread out and Yahweh you shall extol. We shall rejoice and exalt, through Yahshua, who is a descendant of

Peretz. Come in peace, O crown of her Husband, both with songs rejoicing, and gladness among the faithful, the beloved people. Come, O Bride, Come.

It is good to praise Yahweh, and to sing to Your Name, O Most High. To proclaim Your kindness in the morning and Your faithfulness in the night, with ten-stringed instrument and lyre, I sing for joy at the works of Your hand. How great are Your works, Abba Father, how very profound Your thoughts! A brutish man cannot know, a fool cannot comprehend this. When the wicked thrive like grass, and all evildoers flourish-it is in order that they may be destroyed forever. But You Yahweh are exalted forever.

Exalted and hallowed be Your great Name throughout the world which You have created according to Your will. May you establish Your kingdom, bring forth Your redemption and hasten the return of Messiah Yahshua, the Anointed One, in our lifetime and in our days and in The lifetime of the entire house of Israel, speedily and soon. And they shall mourn for Him as for an only child, and in one day, all Israel shall be saved. May His great Name be blessed forever and to all eternity, blessed and praised, glorified, exalted and extolled, honored, adored and lauded be the Name of the

Holy One beyond all the blessing, hymns, praises and consolations that are uttered.

Who is like You among the supernal beings, O Father! Who is like You, resplendent in holiness, awesome in praise, performing wonders! Your children beheld Your sovereignty as you split the sea before Moses. This is my God! They all exclaimed, and declared. Yahweh shall reign forever and ever. Blessed is Yahweh, who has delivered us from bondage.

The children of Israel shall observe the Sabbath establishing the Sabbath throughout their generations as an everlasting covenant. It is a sign between Me and the children of Israel for all time. For in six days Yahweh made the heavens and the earth, and on the seventh day He ceased from work and rested.

Abba Yahweh, open my lips and my mouth shall declare Your praise. Blessed is Yahweh our God and Yahweh of our fathers, God of Abraham, God of Isaac and God of Jacob, the great mighty and awesome God, exalted God, who bestows bountiful kindness, who creates all things, who remembers the piety of the Patriarchs and who, in love, brought the Redeemer to His people for the sake of His Name.

Who is like You, merciful Father, who in compassion remembers His creatures for life. You are holy and Your Name is holy, and the holy Angels praise You daily for all eternity, Blessed is Yahweh, the holy God.

You have consecrated to Your Name the seventh day, the purpose of the creation of heaven and earth. You have blessed it above all days and sanctified it above all festivals. And therefore it is written in Your TORAH.

> The heavens and the earth and all their hosts were completed. And Yahweh finished by the seventh day His work which He had done. And Yahweh blessed the seventh day and made it holy, for on it He rested from all His work which Yahweh created to function.

Those who observe the Sabbath and call it a delight shall rejoice in Your Kingship. The nation which hallows the seventh day shall be satiated and delighted with Your goodness. You called it the most desirable of days, in remembrance of the work of creation.

Yahweh Our God and God of our fathers, please find favor in our rest, make us holy with Your commandments and grant us our portion in the Lamb's Book of Life. Satiate us with Your goodness, gladden our soul with Your salvation, and make our heart pure to serve You in truth. Yahweh our God, grant us our heritage, in love and goodwill, Your holy Sabbath and may all those who sanctify Your Name rest thereon. Blessed is Yahweh who sanctifies the Sabbath.

We thankfully acknowledge that You are Yahweh our God and God of our fathers forever. You are the strength of our life, the shield of our salvation in every generation. We will give thanks to You and recount Your praise, evening, morning and noon, for our lives which are committed into Your hand, for our souls which are entrusted to You, for Your miracles which are with as daily and for Your continual wonders and beneficences, You are the Beneficent One, for Your mercies never cease. And the Merciful One, for Your kindnesses will never end. For we always place our hope in You. And for all these, may Your Name, Yahweh our King, be continually blessed, exalted and extolled forever and ever.

Blessed is Yahweh who blesses His people with peace. May Yahweh guard my tongue from evil and my lips from speaking deceitfully. Let my soul be silent to those who curse me. Let my soul be as dust to all. Open my heart to Your written TORAH, and let my soul eagerly pursue Your commandments. As for all those who plot evil against me, hasten to annul their counsel and frustrate their design. Let them be as chaff before the wind. Let the angel of Yahweh thrust them away that Your beloved ones may be delivered, help us in Yahshua's Name and answer me. Do it for the sake of Your Name. Do it for the sake of Your holiness, do it for the sake of Your right hand. Do it for the sake of Your Word, and do it for the sake of Your Son, Yahshua.

May the words of my mouth and the meditation of my heart be acceptable before You, Yahweh my Strength and my Redeemer. He who makes peace in His heavens, may Yahweh make peace for us and for all Israel. Amen and Amen.

The heavens and the earth and all their hosts were completed. And Yahweh finished by the seventh day His work which He had done, and He rested on the seventh day from all His work which He had done. And Yahweh blessed the seventh day and made it holy, for on it He rested from all His work which Yahweh created to function. Blessed is Yahweh our God and God of our fathers, God of Abraham, God of Isaac and God of Jacob, the great, mighty and awesome God

Yahweh was a shield to our fathers with His word. He resurrects the dead by His utterance. He is the holy God like whom there is none. He gives rest to His people on His holy Sabbath, for to them He desired to give rest. We will serve Him with awe and fear, and offer thanks to His Name every day. Yahweh is the God worthy of thanks, the Master of peace, who sanctifies the Sabbath and blesses the seventh day and brings rest with holiness to a people satiated with delight.

Yahweh, please find favor in our rest. Make us holy with Your commandments and grant us our portion in Your Word. Satiate us with Your goodness, gladden our soul with Your salvation, and make our heart pure to serve You in truth, and Yahweh, our God, grant us our heritage, in love and goodwill, Your holy Sabbath. May Yahweh grant to all those who sanctify Your Name rest thereon. Blessed is Yahweh who sanctifies the Sabbath.

Blessed is Yahweh-Blessed is Yahweh forever and ever.

[Baruch atah Adonai-Baruch atah Adonai l'olam va-ed.]

It is incumbent upon us to praise Yahweh the Master of all things, to exalt the Creator of all existence, that He has not made us like the nations of the world, nor caused us to be like the families of the earth. That He has not assigned us a portion like theirs, or a lot like that of all their multitudes, for they bow to vanity and nothingness. But we bend the knee, bow down, and offer praise before Yahweh the supreme King of kings, the Holy One blessed be He, who stretches forth the heavens and establishes the earth. The seat of whose glory is in the heavens above, and the abode of whose majesty is in the loftiest heights. He is our God, there is none else. Truly, He is our King there is nothing besides Him. Take unto your heart that Yahweh is God, in the heavens above and upon the earth below there is nothing else.

Therefore we hope in You, Abba Father that we may speedily behold the splendor of Your might, to banish idolatry from the earth-and false gods will be utterly destroyed, to perfect the world under the sovereignty of the Almighty. All mankind shall invoke Your Name, to turn to You all the wicked of the earth. Then all the inhabitants of the world will recognize and know that every knee shall bow and every tongue shall confess the Name of Yahweh. Before You, Yahweh our God, they will all take upon themselves the yoke of Your Kingdom. May You soon reign over them forever and ever, for Kingship is Yours, and to all eternity You will reign in glory, as it is written in Your TORAH, Yahweh will reign forever and ever. Yahweh shall be King over the entire earth and His Name One.

Do not fear sudden terror or the destruction of the wicked when it comes. They may contrive a scheme, but it will be foiled. They plot evil against us but it will not materialize, for Yahweh is with us. The righteous will extol Yahweh, the upright will dwell in Your presence forever. To your old age I am with you, and I will carry you, I will sustain you and deliver you.

The sixth day, and the heavens and the earth and all their hosts were completed. And Yahweh finished by the seventh day His work which He had done, and He rested on the seventh day from all His work which He had done. And Yahweh blessed the seventh day and made it holy, for on it He rested from all His work which Yahweh created to function.

[At this time the prayer for the Reading of the Scriptures is offered, followed by a reading of the Scriptures for this Sabbath day. The service is completed with the following.]

For the Scriptures, for the Divine service, for the prophets and for this Sabbath day, which You have given us, Yahweh our God, for sanctity and tranquility, for glory and splendor-for all this, Yahweh our God, we give thanks to You and bless You. May the Name of Yahshua, Your Son, be blessed by the mouth of everyone, constantly and forevermore.

May there come forth from Heaven redemption, grace, kindness compassion, long life, ample sustenance, heavenly assistance, and bodily health, and good vision, healthy and viable children and may the Blessings of Yahweh be upon us all and may Yahweh give us children who will not cease from, nor neglect the words of Scripture. May the King of the universe bless us, prolong our lives, increase our days and lengthen our years. May we be delivered from all distress, all sickness, and all severe afflictions. May Yahweh who is in heaven be our support at all times and seasons.

May Yahwch grant all the desires of our hearts, fulfill all our purposes, and all our petitions. May Yahweh hear from heaven, quickly answer all our requests and save us in the day of trouble. In the Name of Yahshua defend us and send help from heaven to deliver us from bondage, from our enemies and from poverty. B'Shem Yahshua HaMashiach [In the Name of Yahshua the Messiah] we pray. Amen and Amen.

HAVDALAH

(Sabbath Closing)

To light the Sabbath Candles:

> Blessed is Yahweh our God, King of universe, who has sanctified us with Your commandments, and commanded us to kindle the Havdalah light.

> [Baruch atah Adonai eloheinu, melech ha-olam asher kid'shanu b'mitzvotav v'tzivanu l'hadlik ner shel Havdalah.]

Indeed, Yahweh is my deliverance, I am confident and shall not fear, for Yahweh is my strength and song, and He has been a help to me. I shall draw water with joy from the wellsprings of Deliverance. Deliverance is Yahweh's. May Your blessing be upon Your people forever. Yahweh, Lord of hosts is with us, the God of Jacob is our everlasting stronghold. Happy is the man who trusts in You. Abba Father please help us. May the King answer us on the day we call. For the children of Yahweh there is light and joy, gladness and honors-so let it be with us. I raise the cup of deliverance and invoke the Name of Yahweh.

Blessed is Yahweh our God, King of the Universe, Who creates the fruit of the vine.

[Baruch atah Adonai melech ha-olam borei prei ha-gafen.]

Blessed is Yahweh our God, King of the Universe, Who creates the various kinds of spices.

[Baruch atah Adonai melech ha-olam borei minei besamim.]

Blessed is Yahweh our God, King of the Universe, Who creates the lights of fire.

[Baruch atah Adonai melech ha-olam ha-motsea l'kim min ha-aretz.]

Blessed is Yahweh our God, King of the universe, who makes a distinction between the sacred and profane, between light and darkness, between Israel and the nations, between the seventh day and the six work days. Blessed is Yahweh who makes a distinction between the sacred and profane.

May Yahweh open for you His good treasures, the heavens to give rain for your land at its proper time, and to bless all the works of your hands. Yahweh has blessed you as He has promised. Fortunate are the children of Yahweh! Who is like you, a people delivered by Yahweh. You shall tread upon the high places of your enemies. And you will know that I am within My people that I am Yahweh your God, and there is none else.

You will go out with joy, and be led forth in peace, the mountains and the hills will burst into song before you, and all the trees of the field will clap their hands. Indeed, Yahweh is our deliverance, we are confident and shall not fear, for Yahweh is our strength and song, and He has been a help to us.

We will offer thanks to Yahweh, proclaim His Name, make His deeds known among the peoples, cause it to be remembered that the name of Yahweh is exalted. Sing to Yahweh for He has done great things. This is known throughout the earth. Raise your voices joyously and sing for the Holy One is great in your midst. On that day we will say, when we shall look upon His Holy Anointed One, this is our God in whom we have hoped that He should deliver us. This is Yahshua in whom we have hoped. Let us be glad and rejoice in His deliverance.

Yahweh, Creator of the speech of the lips, says, Peace. Peace to him who is far and to him who is near, and I will heal him. And you shall say, May it be so throughout life. May you be at peace, and your household at peace, and all that is yours at peace. Yahweh will give strength to His people, Yahweh will bless His people with peace.

Praise Yahweh, Praise Yahweh from the heavens, praise Him in the celestial heights. Praise Him all His angels; praise Him, all His hosts; praise Him, heaven of heavens, and the waters that are above the heavens. Let them praise the Name of Yahweh, for He commanded and they were created. He has established them forever. For all time He issued a decree, and it shall not be transgressed.

ROSH CHODESH

(New Moon)

(Sound of the Shofar-one long blast)

Blessed is Yahweh our God, King of the Universe, who created the heavens, and with the breath of His mouth, all their hosts. You gave them a set law and time, so that they should not alter their task. They are glad and rejoice to carry out the will of their Creator, the Doer of truth whose Law is the truth. You directed the moon to renew itself as a crown of glory to those who are borne by You from birth, who likewise are destined to be renewed and to glorify their Creator.

Blessed is your Maker. Blessed is He who formed you, blessed is the Creator, blessed is your Master. May all my enemies be unable to touch me harmfully. May there fall upon them terror and dread, by the great strength of Your arm let them be as still as a stone. As a stone let them be quieted by

Your arm's great strength. May dread and terror fall upon them.

Yahshua, the anointed One of Yahweh, son of David, King of Israel, is living and enduring. Peace unto You. May there be good blessings for us and for all of Yahweh's people.

I lift my eyes to the mountains -- from whence comes my help? My help comes from Yahweh, Maker of heaven and earth. He will not let my foot falter, my Guardian does not slumber. Indeed, the Guardian of Israel neither slumbers nor sleeps. Yahweh is my Guardian, Yahweh is my protective shade at my right hand. The sun will not harm me by day, or the moon by night. Yahweh will guard me from all evil, He will guard my soul. Yahweh will guard my going out and my coming in from now and forever.

Praise Yahweh. Praise Yahweh in His Holiness, praise Him in the firmament of His strength, Praise Him for His mighty acts. Praise Him according to His abundant greatness. Praise Him with the sound of the Shofar; praise Him with harp and lyre. Praise Him with timbrel and dance, praise Him with stringed instruments and flute. Praise Him with resounding cymbals, praise Him with clanging cymbals. Let everything that has breath praise Yahweh.

May it be Your will, Yahweh my God and Yahweh of my fathers, to fill the defect of the moon, so that there be no diminution in it, and may the light of the moon be as the light of the sun, as the light of the seven days of creation, as it was before it was diminished, as it is said. And Yahweh made the two great luminaries. May there be fulfilled in us the Scriptural verse which states:

> "They will seek Yahweh their God and Yahshua their King."

May He who performed miracles for our fathers and redeemed them from slavery to freedom, speedily redeem us and gather our dispersed people from the four corners of the earth, and let us say, Amen.

ROSH CHODESH (Name of the new month), will be on (Name of the day of the week on which it falls), which comes to us for good. May the Holy One renew it for us and for all His children, for life and for peace, for gladness and for joy, for deliverance and for consolation, and let us say, Amen.

May our All-Merciful Father Yahweh, who dwells in the supernal heights, in His profound compassion, remember us with mercy. Yahweh is holy and His name is holy, and the holy Angels praise Him daily for all eternity. Blessed is Yahweh, the holy God.

You have given Rosh Chodesh days to Your people, a time of atonement for all their descendants, when they brought before you offerings of goodwill and goats for sin offerings to atone for them. In place of goats and oxen we now have atonement for our sins through the appropriation of the shed Blood of Yahshua. It is a remembrance for us that Yahshua, the Holy Anointed One of God, gave His life as a one-time sacrifice for all time for the atonement of our sins, and as deliverance from the hand of the adversary. Blessed are You, Yahweh our God who has given us His Anointed One Yahshua to make atonement for us.

Yahweh our God and God of our fathers, renew for us this month for good and for blessing, for gladness and for joy, for deliverance and for consolation, for livelihood and for sustenance, for good life and for peace, for the forgiving of sin and the pardoning of our wrongdoing. You have chosen Your people from all nations and established for them the statutes for Rosh Chodesh days. Blessed is Yahweh who sanctifies us and blesses these Rosh Chodesh days.

PESACH

(Passover)

Festival of Freedom

(Nisan 14–21)

Blessed is Yahweh our God, King of the Universe, who performed wondrous deeds for our fathers in olden days, at this season, and for us in times past.

[Baruch atah Adonai eloheinu, melech ha-olam asher kideshanu bemitzvosov vitzivonu lehadlik ner shel sha-bos ve-shel Yom Tov].

Blessed is Yahweh our God, King of the universe who vouchsafed life and health unto us, to behold the return of this festive season.

[Baruch atah Adonai eloheinu, melech ha-olam shehehcheyohnu vikiyoumonu vehegeonu Lizman Hazeh].

Blessed is Yahweh our God, King of the universe, who has sanctified us with His commandments, and has commanded us to kindle the lights of the festival.

[Baruch atah Adonai eloheinu, melech ha-olam, asher kid'shanu b'mitzvotav v'tzivanu l'hadlik ner shel Yom Tov.]

Our Father, our God, with emotions of joy we appear before You to celebrate this great Festival of Freedom. You have redeemed us from slavery, oppression, and bondage and vouchsafed for us liberty and happiness. You have removed the iron yoke of servitude from off our necks, and burst the chains which have fettered us, that we might raise up from despondency to the zealous performance of Your will.

You have chosen us Your people to be the standard bearers of truth, that all men were created free and endowed with inalienable rights. In order to spread this truth, You have scattered us over the face of the earth, to endure trials and persecutions as we battle in service to Your Holy Name. Yet, even in Your mercy You did not forsake us. As you delivered Your people from Egyptian bondage, so in every generation You have been our protector and redeemer, You have been with us in our wanderings, never permitting the waters of oppression to overflow or engulf us. You have been a shield and a protector in our hour of bitter trials. You did not allow the glowing fires of hatred to consume us, but You always preserved us in Your abundant mercy.

In freedom we are able to lift our eyes unto You, Yahweh our God, and bring our tribute of praise and thanksgiving to You who are the Redeemer of mankind and has sent His Holy Anointed One Yahshua, to be the Savior of the world. If You had not been with us when our enemies rose up against us, they would have consumed us. The raging billows of wrath would have overwhelmed us, but for Your merciful kindness in granting our salvation.

Vouchsafe for us these blessings as we celebrate the festival which commemorates Your omnipotence, Your justice and the Sacrifice of Your Holy Anointed One Yahshua, upon the tree, the altar of Your love.

Blessed is Yahweh our God, King of the universe, who has redeemed us from bondage and servitude, and has set us free to worship You.

(The Hallel is said each day of festival.)

SHAVUOT

(Pentecost)

Festival of Weeks

(Sivan 6)

Blessed is Yahweh our God, King of the universe, who performed wondrous deeds for our fathers in olden days, at this season, and for us in times past.

[Baruch atah Adonai eloheinu, melech ha-olam asher kideshanu bemitzvosov vitzivonu lehadlik ner shel sha-bos ve-shel Yom Tov].

Blessed is Yahweh our God, King of the universe who vouchsafed life and health unto us, to behold the return of this festive season.

[Baruch atah Adonai eloheinu, melech ha-olam shehehcheyohnu vikiyoumonu vehegeonu Lizman Hazeh].

Blessed is Yahweh our God, King of the universe, who has sanctified us with His commandments, and has commanded us to kindle the lights of the festival.

[Baruch atah Adonai eloheinu, melech ha-olam, asher kid'shanu b'mitzvotav v'tzivanu l'hadlik ner shel Yom Tov.]

Abba Father, Yahweh our God, we remember in times past how as we wondered in the wilderness of Sinai, before the mount of Sinai, You appeared before Your people and gave us Your Commandments, as it is written:

You shall have no other gods before me.

You shall not make for yourselves any graven image, or any likeness that is in heaven above, or that is in the earth. You shall not bow down to them, nor serve them, for I Yahweh your God am a jealous God.

You shall not take the Name of Yahweh your God in vain, for Yahweh will not hold him guiltless that takes His Name in vain.

Remember the Sabbath to keep it holy. Six days you shall labor, and do all your work, but the seventh day is the Sabbath of Yahweh your God, in it you shall not do any work, for in six days Yahweh made heaven and earth, the sea, and all that is in them, and rested the seventh day, wherefore Yahweh blessed the Sabbath, and hallowed it.

Honor your father and your mother, that your days may be long upon the land which Yahweh your God gives you.

You shall not kill (murder).

You shall not commit adultery.

You shall not steal.

You shall not bear false witness against your neighbor.

You shall not covet your neighbor's house; you shall not covet your neighbor's wife, or his manservant, or his maidservant, or his ox, or his ass, or anything that is your neighbor's.

And all the people saw the thundering, and the lightings, and the noise of the Shofar, and the mountain smoking and when the people saw it, they removed, and stood afar off. And they said unto Moses, "Speak with us, and we will hear, but let not Yahweh speak with us lest we die." And Moses said unto the people, "Fear not, for Yahweh is come to prove you that His Fear may be before your faces that you sin not."

And Yahweh our God spoke to us out of the cloud and said, Hear therefore, O Israel, and observe to do it, that it may be well with you, and that you may increase mightily. You shall observe to do as Yahweh your God has commanded you that you may live, and that it may be well with you, and that you may prolong your days in the land which you shall possess.

Hear, O Israel, Yahweh our God is one, and you shall love Yahweh your God with all your heart, and with all your soul, and with all your might. And these words, which I command you this day, shall be in your heart, and you shall teach them diligently unto your children, and shall talk of them when you sit in your house, and when you walk by the way, and when you lie down, and when you rise up. And you shall bind them for a sign upon your hand and they shall be as reminders between your eyes. And you shall write them upon the doorposts of your house, and on your gates.

Now therefore, if you will obey My voice indeed, and keep My Covenant, then you shall be a peculiar treasure unto Me above all people, for all the earth is Mine, and you shall be unto Me a kingdom of priests, and a holy nation. These are the words which you shall speak unto the children of Israel. And all the people answered together, and said, "All that Yahweh has spoken we will do."

A Psalm of David. The Law of Yahweh is perfect, converting the soul, the testimony of Yahweh is sure making wise the simple. The statutes of Yahweh are right, rejoicing the heart. The Commandment of Yahweh is pure, enlightening the eyes. The fear of Yahweh is clean, enduring forever, the judgments of Yahweh are true and righteous altogether. More to be desired are they than gold, yea, than much fine gold, sweeter also than honey and the honeycomb. Moreover by them is your servant warned, and in keeping of them is great reward.

Let the words of my mouth, and the meditation of heart, be acceptable in your sight, Abba Father, my strength, and my redeemer.

Blessed is Yahweh our God, King of the universe, who has sanctified us by His

Commandments and commanded us to obey His Holy Word.

Blessed is Yahweh our God, King of the universe, who has given us His Holy Scriptures.

Our Father Yahweh, we remember in times past how on the day of Pentecost (Shavuot), You sent Your Holy Spirit upon Your servants and anointed them with power from on high, as it was written. "And it shall come to pass afterward, I will pour out My Spirit upon all flesh, and your sons and your daughters shall prophesy, your old men shall dream dreams, your young men shall see visions and also upon the servants and upon the handmaids in those days will I pour out My Spirit."

And it shall come to pass, that whoever shall call on the Name of Yahweh shall be delivered, for in Mount Zion and in Jerusalem shall be deliverance, as Yahweh has said, and in the remnant whom Yahweh shall call. Blessed is Yahweh our God, King of the Universe, who by Your Holy Anointed One, Yahshua, promised to send Your Holy Spirit to guide us, to teach us, to empower us to keep the Law, and to bear witness to Yahshua the Messiah, son of David and High Priest of Yahweh.

May the possession of the written TORAH fill us with gladness, that we may bear in mind that it is our life, the source of our continued existence, and that we may ever be anxious to devote to it our brightest hours. But never, Yahweh our Father, withdraw Your love from us that we may be empowered by Your Holy Spirit to fulfill our divine mission to teach all nations and to baptize them in the Name of Yahshua for the remission of sin, so that they likewise may be saved and receive the baptism of the Holy Spirit and walk in the light of Your righteous Commandments. Blessed is Yahweh our God, King of the universe, who fulfills His every promise.

(The Hallel is said each day of festival.)

ROSH HASHANAH

(New Year)

(Tishrei 1)

Prayer for New Year's Eve:

Blessed is Yahweh our God, King of the universe who vouchsafed life and health unto us, to behold the return of this festive season.

[Baruch atah Adonai eloheinu, melech ha-olam shehehcheyohnu vikiyoumonu vehegeonu Lizman Hazeh].

Blessed is Yahweh our God, King of the universe, who has sanctified us with His commandments, and has commanded us to kindle the lights of the festival.

[Baruch atah Adonai eloheinu, melech ha-olam, ashcr kid'shanu b'mitzvotav v'tzivanu l'hadlikner shel Yom Tov.]

Our heavenly Father, out of the depths of our hearts we call upon You to hear our Prayer and to accept our supplications. We come before You this night to render praise and adoration unto Your Name. We bring unto You the thankful offerings of our lips for the numberless blessings from Your bounty, and we beseech You to grant us in the coming year life and prosperity, blessings and contentment.

We have come with trust in Your mercy, and we wait upon You as children wait for their father's blessings. As we look back over the past year and see the many joys and pains it has brought, we also look forward into the darkness of the future New Year, considering what joys and sorrows it may contain for us. We perceive and acknowledge that our destinies are in Your hand, and that mercy and kindness are with You. Therefore, we put our trust in You, we pour out our souls before You as we are overwhelmed by our emotions of expectations and fears.

Be pleased to accept the thanks which we render unto You for the many joys, the many consolations, the many blessings You have bestowed upon us during the past year. Accept also the thanks we render to You, even for the trials with which You visited upon us, for the sorrows which You saw fit to afflict us with, the grievous burdens You have placed upon us, in order that we might be cleansed and purified from all that is sinful and debasing, and be led in meekness unto You Yahweh, our Lord and our Master.

Father we pray that you would look upon us with grace in the coming New Year. Let the abundance of Your blessings rest upon us, that it may become a year of life and health to all that call upon You. That the New Year may be a year in which Your holy Anointed One Yahshua may be revealed in the midst of Israel. That it may be a year of increased love and fear of Your holy Name and of our esteem and appreciation for Your mighty works.

Grant, heavenly Father, that everywhere Your children may be relieved of the heavy and painful burden of oppression which has its origin in days of prejudice. Grant that barriers may be torn down which separate Your people. Grant unto us Father that the knowledge of Your Name and the Name of

Your Anointed One, Yahshua our Messiah, may be enkindled, and shine resplendent. Destroy the seeds of discord which diminish the light of Your countenance within us, and limit the impact of Your message of redemption and salvation to the entire world.

Our Father, You are the Judge of our actions, and our deeds lie open before You like an open book. Judge us not according to our deeds, but let Your grace reign over us. Forgive us our failings and pardon our sins. When You pass judgment upon us, let us appear before you cleansed and purified by the shed Blood of Yahshua, the Lamb of Yahweh who takes away the sins of the world. For You are the God of love and mercy, and in the Name of Yahshua there is redemption. Grant that the sound of the Shofar may enter into our hearts, and awaken in us all the noble resolves and vows to which Your voice has summoned us, and like those who have gone before us, let us exclaim, "Whatever Yahweh requires of us, we will do in humble obedience to His Word."

We call forth the Seven Remembrances which You enjoined Upon us:

Remember the day you came out of Egypt all the days of your life. But beware and guard your souls carefully lest you forget the things which your eyes have seen, and lest they be removed from your heart. Make known to your children what you saw on the day when you stood before Yahweh your Yahweh at Mount Sinai.

Remember what Amalek did to you on the way as you came out of Egypt. How he met you on the way, and cut down all the weak who straggled behind you, when you were weary and exhausted, and he did not fear Yahweh. Therefore, when Yahweh your God will relieve you of all your enemies around you in the land which Yahweh your God gives you as a hereditary portion, you shall blot out the memory of Amalek from under heaven. Do not forget.

Remember and do not forget how you provoked Yahweh your God to wrath in the desert.

Remember what Yahweh did to Miriam on the way, as you came out of Egypt.

Remember the Sabbath day to keep it holy.

Remember Yahshua, the Holy Anointed One of Yahweh, who was slain and lives again to make intercession for us before Yahweh our God.

A Psalm of David: Yahweh is our Shepherd, we shall not want. Yahweh makes us to lie down in green pastures. He leads us beside the still waters. Yahweh restores our souls. He leads us in the paths of righteousness for His Name's sake. Yea, though we walk through the valley of the shadow of death, we will fear no evil, for Yahweh is with us. Your rod, Father, and Your staff they comfort us. Yahweh prepares a table before us in the presence of our enemies. Yahweh anoints our heads with oil, our cups run over. Surely goodness and mercy shall follow us all the days of our lives, and we shall dwell in the house of Yahweh forever.

Prayer for the New Year's Day

Yahweh our God and God of our fathers, as Abraham, willing to sacrifice his son Isaac, overcame his sense of compassion to do Your will, so may Your love of compassion overwhelm Your demand for strict judgment. Show mercy and remove sorrow and distress from Your people. Fulfill Your promise in the Scriptures. “I will remember My Covenant with Jacob, My Covenant with Isaac, My Covenant with Abraham, and I will remember My Covenant with Mine Anointed One Yahshua, son of David.

Blessed is Yahweh our God, King of the universe, who has sanctified us with His Commandments, and commanded us to hear the sound of the Shofar.

Blessed is Yahweh our God, King of the universe, who granted us life, who sustained us, and who enabled us to reach this day.

The Shofar is sounded:

Tekiah = one long blast (8 seconds)

Teruah = 9 short staccato blasts

Shevarim = 3 blasts somewhat longer than Teruah

TEKIAH SHEVARIM-TERUAH TEKIAH

TEKIAH SHEVARIM TEKIAH

TEKIAH TERUAH TEKIAH

TEKIAH TERUAH TEKIAH

Fortunate are the people who know the sound of the Shofar. They walk in the light of Your countenance. They rejoice in Your Name, and are exalted through Your righteousness.

Here I stand, impoverished in merit, trembling in Your Presence, pleading on behalf of Your people, even though I am unfit and unworthy. Therefore, gracious and compassionate Father, Awesome God of Abraham, in Yahshua's name, I plead for help as I seek mercy for myself and for my family. Charge them not for my sins. May they not be ashamed for my deeds, and may their deeds cause me no shame. Accept my Prayer as the Prayer of Your Holy One, Yahshua, son of David and High Priest of God.

Remove all obstacles and adversaries, draw Your veil of love over all our faults, transform our afflictions into joy and gladness, life and peace. May we always love truth and peace. And may no obstacles hinder our Prayers.

Revered, exalted, awesome God, may my Prayer reach You for the sake of all honest, pious, righteous men, for the sake of Your glory, and for the sake of Your Son, Yahshua. Master of the universe, if we do not possess meritorious deeds, let the great Name of Your Anointed One stand up in our behalf and do not enter into judgment with us.

Yahweh listens to the needy and hears entreaties. He extends His goodwill and curtails His wrath. He is the first of all that was, and the last of all who will ever be, He will reign forever and ever.

Holy congregations sanctify aloud, myriads of angels sing aloud. Yahweh is King, Yahweh was King, and Yahweh shall be King forever.

You are holy and Your Name is holy, and holy Angels praise You daily for all eternity. All generations shall proclaim the Kingship of Yahweh, for He alone is exalted and holy. And thus shall your Name, Yahweh our God, be sanctified upon Your people, upon the Kingship of the house of David, upon Yahshua, Your Anointed, and upon Your sanctuary. Our Father, our King, we have no King but You.

Our Father, act benevolently with us for the sake of Yahshua Your Anointed One, and renew for us a good year.

Our Father, our King, destroy every oppressor and adversary from against us, and close the mouths of our adversaries and accusers.

Our Father, our King, remove pestilence, sword, famine, captivity and destruction from us and withhold the plague from our dwellings.

Our Father, our King, bring us back to You in wholehearted repentance, and send complete healing to the sick of Your people. Yahweh rend the evil aspect of the verdict decreed against us, and remember us with a favorable remembrance before You.

Our Father, our King, inscribe us in the book of good life, and in the book of redemption and deliverance.

Our Father, out King, inscribe us in the book of livelihood and sustenance, and cause deliverance to flourish for us soon.

Our Father, our King, exalt the glory of Your people, and exalt the glory of Your Anointed One, Yahshua, son of David and High Priest of God.

Our Father, our King, fill our hands with Your blessings, and fill our storehouses with plenty.

Our Father, our King, have pity and compassion upon us, and accept our Prayer with mercy and with favor. Open the gates of heaven and do not turn us away from You empty handed.

Our Father, our King, may this be an hour of mercy and a time of favor before You. Have compassion upon us, and upon our children.

Our Father, our King, do it for the sake of Your Anointed One, Yahshua, who was sacrificed for Your Holy Name, and for our salvation. Do it for the sake of those who suffered through fire and affliction for the sanctification of Your Name.

Our Father, our King, avenge the spilled blood of Your servants. Do it for Your sake, if not for ours, and deliver us. Do it for the sake of Your abounding mercies.

Our Father, our King, do it for the sake of Your great, mighty and Awesome Name Yahweh which is proclaimed over us, and be gracious to us, for we have no meritorious deeds, deal charitably and kindly with us and deliver us.

Bestow peace, goodness, blessing, life, graciousness, kindness and mercy, upon us and upon all Your people. Bless us, our Father, with the light of Your countenance. For by the light of Your countenance, You gave us the Word of Life. May it be favorable in Your eyes to bless us at all times and at every moment with Your peace and Your Presence.

And may we be found, Yahweh our God, in the Lamb's Book of Life, for blessing, peace and decrees. May we and all Your people be remembered and inscribed before You for a happy life and for peace. May our Prayers and our supplications be accepted before You in heaven. May there be abundant peace from heaven and a good life for us and for all of Yahweh's people. May He who makes peace in His heavens make peace for us. Amen and Amen.

YOM KIPPUR

(Day of Atonement)

(Tishrei 10)

Blessed is Yahweh our God, King of the universe, who has sanctified us with His commandments, and has commanded us to kindle the lights of the festival.

[Baruch atah Adonai eloheinu, melech ha-olam, asher kid'shanu b'mitzvotav v'tzivanu l'hadlik ner shel Yom Tov.]

Our God, and God of our fathers, may our prayers come before You. Hide not from our supplications for we are neither so arrogant nor so hardened as to say before You, Yahweh our God and God of our fathers, that we are righteous and have not sinned, for verily we have sinned.

We have transgressed, we have dealt treacherously, we have robbed, we have slandered, we have acted perversely, and we have wrought wickedness, we have been presumptuous, we have done violence, we have lied, we have counseled evil, we have spoken falsely, we have scoffed, we have rebelled, we have provoked, we have committed iniquity, and we have oppressed, we have been stiff-necked, we have done wickedly, we have corrupted, we have committed abominations, we have gone astray, we have led others astray.

We have turned away from Your commandments and Your judgments that are good, and it has profited us nothing. But You are righteous in all that has come upon us for You have acted truthfully, but we have wrought unrighteousness. What shall we say before You who dwell on high and what shall we declare before You who abides in the heavens? You know the mysteries of the universe and the hidden secrets of all living. You search out the heart of man, and probe all our thoughts and aspirations, Nothing escapes You, neither is anything concealed from Your might. May it be Your will, Yahweh our God and God of our fathers, to forgive us in Yahshua's Name all our sins, to pardon all our transgressions:

[For each declaration smite your heart with your right hand as you make the confession.]

For the sin which we have committed against You, under compulsion or of our own will, and by the hardening of our hearts.

For the sin which we have committed against You, unknowingly.

For the sin which we have committed against You, by unchastely.

For the sin which we have committed against You, knowingly and deceitfully.

For the sin which we have committed against You, by wrong doing.

For the sin which we have committed against You, by association.

For the sin which we have committed against You, by doubt and unbelief.

For the sin which we have committed against You, in presumption, in error, or by violence.

For the sin which we have committed against You, by the profanation of Your Holy Name.

For the sin which we have committed against You, by the evil inclination, or unwittingly.

For the sin which we have committed against You, by denial and lying.

For the sin which we have committed against You, by scoffing and slander.

For the sin which we have committed against You, by stretching forth the neck in pride.

For all of these, Yahweh, Lord God of forgiveness, forgive us, pardon us, and grant us atonement through the Name and shed Blood of Your Holy Anointed One Yahshua, son of David, and High Priest of Yahweh.

For the sin which we have committed against You, by haughty eyes and by effrontery.

For the sin which we have committed against You, by casting off the yoke of Your Commandments.

For the sin which we have committed against You, by ensnaring our neighbor, by envy and by being contentious.

For the sin which we have committed against You, by doing evil.

For the sin which we have committed against You, by tale bearing, by vain oaths, and by causeless hatred.

For the sin which we have committed against You, by breach of trust. For all of these, Yahweh Lord God of forgiveness, forgive us, pardon us, and grant us atonement in the Name and by the shed Blood of Your Holy Anointed One Yahshua, son of David and High Priest of Yahweh.

Yahweh, God of our fathers, who gives salvation to nations and strength to governments, may our Prayers come before You. Hide not

Yourself from our supplications for our country, for we have trespassed, we have dealt treacherously, we have robbed, we have slandered, we have acted perversely, and we have wrought wickedness in the land, we have been presumptuous, we have done violently, we have framed lies, we have counseled evil, and we have dealt falsely, we have been proud, we have scoffed, we have provoked and we have revolted and rebelled against You. We have oppressed, we have been stiff-necked, we have been corrupt, and we have committed abominations, we have gone astray and we have led others astray.

We have turned away from Your commandments and Your judgments and we have wrought all kinds of unrighteousness in the land which You have given us. You know the mysteries of the universe and the hidden secrets of all living. May it be Your will, Yahweh our God and God of our fathers, to forgive us and to grant us atonement in the Name and by the shed Blood of Your Holy Anointed One Yahshua, son of David and High Priest of God, to forgive us for all the sins of the nation which we have wrought. May it be Your will our Father to bless and safeguard our country, and the people who live here. May brotherly love be found among all the people.

Yahweh our God, and God of our fathers, protect and help us. Give us leaders who will honor Your Name and obey Your Commandments. Grant them wisdom and understanding that they may lead our nation in justice and righteousness. May it be Your will that the dominion of tyranny and cruelty speedily be brought to an end and the Kingdom of righteousness be established upon the earth with liberty and freedom for all mankind.

Blessed is Yahweh our God, and God of Abraham, God of Isaac, and God of Jacob, the great, almighty, revered and exalted God who bestows loving-kindness, have mercy upon us and upon our children and upon all who revere Your Holy Name. Yahweh send Your Holy Anointed One Yahshua to bring us deliverance and eternal salvation.

With trepidation in my heart for the people of this nation and for the sins that have been wrought, I offer grievous supplications, bending the knee as I bear my country's message. You have brought me forth from the womb, enlighten the darkness which covers our land, that I may speak words of favor, and lead me in Your truth. Teach me to pour forth inspiring meditation, shelter me under Your protection and draw me close to You. My cries come from the depths of my soul. Let Your love in judgment be near at hand. Teach me to pray with understanding, that I may bring healing to our beloved land, and to Your people. Prepare my way that my speech will not falter, support my steps lest they fail, uphold and strengthen me that I may not grow weary or faint, accept my words and suffer me not to fall. From terror and trembling preserve me, regard my contrition and come to my assistance.

Yahweh our Father gives food unto all creatures grant that I and my family may likewise find needful support of life. I pray not for great riches or possessions, but give me, Father, what I need, and what is good and beneficial for me. Keep me and my family from want and privation, and direct our hearts that in the pursuit for the necessities of life, we may never deviate from the path of righteousness.

Vouchsafe for us the means of helping the poor and needy, according to the best impulses of our hearts, and let our home ever be open to the distressed and the afflicted, that they may find comfort and relief.

Be pleased heavenly Father to grant unto all my family the blessings of health, keep far from us sickness and sorrow. Preserve my wife unto me in life and health. Keep watch over our domestic happiness and peace, and grant eternal salvation through the Name of Yahshua. Bountiful Father, bless and preserve this family that it may grow in happiness, realizing our hopes, and glorifying Your Name. In Yahshua's Name I pray. Amen and Amen.

SUKKOT

(Feast of Tabernacles & Yahshua's Birthday)

(Tishrei 14-22)

Blessed is Yahweh our God, King of the universe, who has vouchsafed life and health unto us, to behold the return of this festive season.

[Baruch atah Adonai eloheinu, melech ha-olam she-heh-che-yoh-nu vee-kee-mo-nu ve-he-ge-o-nu liz-man ha-zeh.]

Blessed is Yahweh our God, King of the universe, who has sanctified us with His commandments, and has commanded us to kindle the lights of the festival.

[Baruch atah Adonai eloheinu, melech ha-olam, asher kid'shanu b'mitzvotav v'tzivanu l'hadlik ner shel Yom Tov.]

To the children of Israel this is a time of remembrance wherein our fathers dwelt in tents for forty years in the wilderness, when our nation trustfully followed Yahweh our God. This remains as a period which continues to illustrate that You are the Leader and Educator of all mankind. As our fathers were, so are we witnesses of Your divine providence, and we are the herald of Your bountiful government on earth. Like them we have passed through many inhospitable wildernesses, through the desert and wasteland, with the blazing pillar of Your Law illuminating our paths in the darkness of sorrow and distress and the pillar of cloud of Your mercy sheltering us from the scorching rays of trouble and danger.

We are witnesses of Your preserving and sustaining mercy and kindness. You did not allow us to perish for the sake of Your great Name and Your holy Law. The Feast of Tabernacles is a feast of thanksgiving for Your merciful blessings and paternal protection.

This is a feast of admonition to continually work for the glorification of Your Holy Name Yahweh. This is also a feast of trust, that as in the past You sent forth Your Anointed One Yahshua to tabernacle among us. Yahshua, the Messiah was born on the first day of this festival. We are reminded that Yahshua was Immanuel, that is, Yahweh is with us. And we beheld Him, the only begotten of the Father, and on the eighth day of His birth, the temple of His body was dedicated, as it is written, "For mine eyes have seen Your salvation, which You have prepared before Your people, a light to lighten the Gentiles, and the glory of Your people Israel.

(The Hallel is said each day of festival.)

Law of The Lulav

Blessed is Yahweh our God, King of the universe who has sanctified us with His commandments, and has commanded us concerning the taking of a palm branch.

[Baruch atah Adonai eloheinu, melech ha-olam asher kid'shanu b'mitzvotav v'tzivanu al ne-teelas Lulav.]

The Lulav (Palm Branch)

The Hadassim (Myrtles.)

Aravot (Willows)

All of these shall be bound and tied together. When holding them, the spine or back (Shedrah) of the Lulav (Palm Branch) shall be towards one's face. The Hadassim (Myrtle) are to be placed on the right side of the Shedrah (Spine) of the Lulav (palm Branch).

The two Aravot (Willows) are to be placed to the left of the Shedrah (Spine) of the Lulav (Palm Branch).

The Baruchah (Blessing) of the Lulav shall be said after the Amidah (Silent) Prayer, and before pronouncing the Hallel. One should say the Baruchah (Blessing) in the morning in the Sukkah (Booth).

The Lulav is bound together with the Hadassim and the Aravot and taken in the right hand and the Baruchah (Blessing) is said' The Etrog (citrus Fruit) is taken in the left hand and is brought together with the Lulav, at the bottom of the Lulav, Hadassim and Aravot. They are moved in six directions, a total of eighteen movements, i.e., three times to and fro in each direction. Each time the four species are brought back, their lower tips should actually touch the chest. When making the movement forward, care should be taken that the top of the Lulav should not touch the wall or the top of the Succoth.

Facing east, the order of the six movements are:

The first to the South,

the second to the North,

the third to the East,

the fourth upward,

the fifth downward (however, the Lulav should not be inverted, rather the movement of the hands should be downward and upward. Likewise, in all movements, the Lulav shall be held upwards, and only the hands holding the four species should be moved toward the specific direction.

The sixth movement is made over the right shoulder towards the West.

The Blessing is said just prior to the waving of the Lulav every day except on the Sabbath. The Lulav is not waved on the Sabbath.

SIMCHAT TORAH

(Tishrei 23)

(The written TORAH scrolls are carried around the BIMAH (Ark) seven times, with dancing and singing. We complete the cycle of TORAH reading with the last chapter of Deuteronomy and begin immediately anew with Genesis, chapter 1, verse 1).

And on the eighth day a holy convocation was held to review the festive gatherings of this month, the lessons which they have taught, and the sacred emotions which they have aroused, the thoughts of repentance which they have evoked, the tidings of forgiveness which they have proclaimed, and the joyous and grateful recollections which they have awaken, the fervent prayers which they have inspired-that we may once more, collect our thoughts in Your presence, and seriously examine the results of our frequent convocation for divine worship in Your house.

You have ordained that these sacred days of contemplation and repentance should be followed by days of thanksgiving and rejoicing at the birth of Your Holy Anointed One Yahshua, in order that we may feel the happiness You have imparted to us, and in which we share with You, Yahweh our God.

Let not the lessons of our sacred days and the birth of the Messiah Yahshua, pass by unheeded. Let the ennoblement of our hearts and the purification of our souls be our harvest. Bless the work of our hands, grant full and ample success to all our undertakings.

Let a joyous and contented spirit prevail in our families, and keep us far removed from trials, misfortunes, grief and affliction. And throughout all the days of our lives, we will render praise unto You Yahweh, who has appointed Your festivals to consecrate, sanctify and memorialize the birth, life, death, and resurrection of the Holy Anointed One Yahshua, son of David and High Priest of Yahweh.

Instill in us the desire to labor for all the works of holiness, and for the happiness of Your people, and all mankind. May our festivals, which commemorate Your Son Yahshua, confirm within us the belief in Your bountiful providence, and cause us to devote our lives into Your service.

Blessed is Yahweh our God, unto whom all praise belongs, now and forevermore. Yahweh shall reign forever and ever.

HALLEL

The Hallel is recited the first two days of Passover [Pesach] and Pentecost [Shavuot]; each of the nine days of the Feast of Tabernacles [Sukkot], and the eight days of the Feast of Lights and Dedication [Chanukah].

Praise Yahweh. Praise the name of Yahweh. Blessed is the name of Yahweh from this time forth and for evermore. From the rising of the sun unto the going down of the same Yahweh's name is to be praised. Yahweh is high above all nations, and His glory above the heavens. Who is like unto Yahweh our God, who dwells on High. Who humbles himself to behold the things that are in heaven, and in the earth! He raises up the poor out of the dust, and lifts the needy out of the dunghill, that he may set him with princes, even with the princes of his people. He maketh the barren woman to keep house, and to be a joyful mother of children. Praise Yahweh.

When Israel went out of Egypt, the house of Jacob from a people of strange language; Judah was his sanctuary, and Israel his dominion. The sea saw it, and fled. Jordan was driven back. The mountains skipped like rams, and the little hills like lambs. What ailed you, O sea that you fled? River Jordan, that you were driven back? You mountains that you skipped like rams; and you little hills, like lambs? Tremble, you earth, at the presence of Yahweh, at the presence of the God of Jacob; who turned the rock into standing water, the flint into a fountain of waters.

Not unto us, Abba Father, not unto us, but unto Your name give glory, for Your mercy, and for Your truth's sake. Wherefore should the heathen say, "Where is their God?" Our God is in the heavens; He has done whatsoever He has pleased. Their idols are silver and gold, the work of men's hands. They have mouths, but they speak not, eyes have they, but they see not. They have ears, but they hear not, noses have they, but they smell not. They have hands, but they handle not, feet have they, but they walk not, neither do they speak through their throat. They that make them are like unto them; so is every one that trusted in them.

O Israel, trust in Yahweh your God. He is your help and your shield. O house of Aaron, trust in Yahweh, He is your help and your shield. You that fear Yahweh, trust in Yahweh. He is our help and our shield.

Yahweh has been mindful of us. He will bless us; He will bless the house of Israel; he will bless the house of Aaron. He will bless them that fear Yahweh, both small and great. Yahweh shall increase us more and more, we and our children.

We are blessed of Yahweh which made heaven and earth. The heaven, even the heavens, are Yahweh's, but the earth has He given to the children of men. The dead praise not Yahweh, neither any that go down into silence. But we will bless Yahweh from this time forth and for evermore. Praise Yahweh.

I love Yahweh, because He has heard my voice and my supplications. Because He has inclined His ear unto me, therefore will I call upon Him as long as I live. The sorrows of death compassed me, and the pains of hell got hold upon me, I found trouble and sorrow. Then called I upon the name of Yahweh; Abba Father, I beseech You, deliver my soul. Gracious is Yahweh, and righteous, yes, our God is merciful.

Yahweh preserves the simple, I was brought low, and He helped me. Return unto your rest, O my soul for Yahweh has dealt bountifully with me. Yahweh has delivered my soul from death, my eyes from tears, and my feet from falling. I will walk before Yahweh in the land of the living. I believed, therefore have I spoken. I was greatly afflicted. I said in my haste, "All men are liars. What shall I render unto Yahweh for all His benefits toward me? I will take the cup of salvation, and call upon the name of Yahweh. I will pay my vows unto Yahweh now in the presence of all His people." Precious in the sight of Yahweh is the death of his saints.

Abba Father, truly I am Your servant. I am Your servant, and the son of Your handmaid. You have loosed my bonds. I will offer to You the sacrifice of thanksgiving, and will call upon the name of Yahweh. I will pay my vows unto Yahweh now in the presence of all His people, in the courts of Yahweh's house, in the midst of you, O Jerusalem. Praise Yahweh.

O Praise Yahweh, all you nations, praise Him, all you people. For His merciful kindness is great towards us and the truth of Yahweh endures forever. Praise Yahweh.

O give thanks unto Yahweh, for He is good, because His mercy endures forever. Let Israel now say, that His mercy endures forever. Let the house of Aaron now say, that His mercy endures forever. Let them now that fear Yahweh say, that His mercy endures forever. I called upon Yahweh in my distress. Yahweh answered me, and set me in a large place. Yahweh is on my side; I will not fear, what can man do to me? Yahweh takes my part with them that help me. Therefore shall I see my desire upon them that hate me. It is better to trust in Yahweh than to put confidence in man. It is better to trust in Yahweh than to put confidence in princes. All nations compassed me about, but in the name of Yahweh I will destroy them. They compassed me about, yes, they compassed me about, but in the name of Yahweh I will destroy them. They compassed me about like bees; they are quenched as the fire of thorns, for in the name of Yahweh I will destroy them. They have thrust sore at me that I might fall, but Yahweh helped me.

Yahweh is my strength and song, and is become my salvation. The voice of rejoicing and salvation is in the tabernacles of the righteous. The right hand of Yahweh does valiantly. The right hand of Yahweh is exalted. I shall not die, but live, and declare the works of Yahweh. Yahweh has chastened me sore, but He has not given me over unto death.

Open to me the gates of righteousness. I will go into them, and I will praise Yahweh, this gate of Yahweh into which the righteous shall enter. Abba Father, I will praise You, for You have heard me, and have become my salvation.

The stone which the builders refused is become the head stone of the corner. This is Yahweh's doing; it is marvelous in our eyes. This is the day which Yahweh has made; we will rejoice and be glad in it. Save now, I beseech You, Abba Father, I beseech You, send now prosperity.

Blessed is He that comes in the name of Yahweh. We have blessed You out of the house of Yahweh. Yahweh is God, who has showed us light. Bind the sacrifice with cords, even unto the horns of the altar. You are my God, and I will praise You. You are my God, I will exalt You. O give thanks unto Yahweh; for He is good, for His mercy endures forever. Praise Yahweh.

Praise Yahweh O my soul. While I live will I praise Yahweh, I will sing praises unto Yahweh while I have any being. Put not your trust in princes, or in the son of man, in whom there is no help. His breath goes forth, he returns to his earth. In that very day his thoughts perish. Happy is he that has Yahweh, the God of Jacob for his help, whose hope is in Yahweh his God, which made heaven, and earth, the sea, and all that therein is; which keeps truth forever, which executes judgment for the oppressed which gives food to the hungry.

Yahweh loses the prisoners Yahweh opens the eyes of the blind. Yahweh raises them that are bowed down; Yahweh loves the righteous; Yahweh preserves the strangers; He relieves the fatherless and widow, but the way of the wicked he turns upside down. Yahweh shall reign forever, even your God, O Zion, unto all generations. Praise Yahweh.

Praise Yahweh. Praise Yahweh from the heavens, praise Him in the heights. Praise Him all His angels, praise Him all His hosts. Praise Him sun and moon; praise Him all you stars of light. Praise Him, you heavens of heavens, and you waters that be above the heavens. Let them praise the name of Yahweh for He commanded and they were created. He has also established them forever and ever. He has made a decree which shall not pass.

Praise Yahweh from the earth you dragons and all deeps; fire, and hail; snow and vapors;

stormy wind fulfilling His word. Mountains and all hills; fruitful trees and all cedars; beasts and all cattle; creeping things and flying fowl; kings of the earth and all people; princes and all judges of the earth; both young men and maidens; old men and children. Let them praise the name of Yahweh for His name alone is excellent, His glory is above the earth and heaven. He also exalts the horn of His people, the praise of all His saints; even of the children of Israel, a people near unto Him. Praise Yahweh.

Praise Yahweh. Sing unto Yahweh a new song, and His praise in the congregation of saints. Let Israel rejoice in Him that made him, let the children of Zion be joyful in their King. Let them praise His name in the dances, let them sing praises unto Him with the timbre and harp. For Yahweh takes pleasure in His people, He will beautify the meek with salvation. Let the saints be joyful in glory let them sing aloud upon their beds. Let the high praises of Yahweh be in their mouth, and a two-edged sword in their hand; to execute vengeance upon the heathen, and punishments upon the people; to bind their kings with chains, and their nobles with fetters of iron; to execute upon them the judgment written, this honor have all his saints.

Praise Yahweh. Praise Yahweh in His sanctuary; praise Him in the firmament of His power. Praise Him for His mighty acts praise Him according to His excellent greatness. Praise Him with the sound of the trumpet; praise Him with the psaltery and harp. Praise Him with the timbre and dance; praise Him with stringed instruments and organs. Praise Him upon the loud cymbals; praise Him upon the high sounding cymbals. Let everything that has breath praise Yahweh.

CHANUKAH

(Festival of Lights and Dedication)

(Kislev 25-Tevet 3)

Blessed is Yahweh our God, King of the universe who vouchsafed life and health unto us, to behold the return of this festive season.

[Baruch atah Adonai eloheinu, melech ha-olam she-heh-che-yoh-nu vee-kee-mo-nu ve-he-ge-onu liz-man ha-zeh.]

Heavenly Father, throughout history Your children have been plunged into deepest darkness, but we have endured. The light of our faith still burns brightly within our hearts, and once again, with Your help, we have survived. Now, as we kindle the lights of Chanukah, let these lights affirm our faith in You our Father, and in Your Holy Anointed One Yahshua. May they illumine our lives even as they fill us with gratitude that we have been saved from our enemies.

[The candles are placed in the Menorah from right to left, and kindled from left to right.]

Blessed is Yahweh our God, King of universe, who has sanctified us with His commandments, and commanded us to kindle the Chanukah Lights.

[Baruch atah Adonai eloheinu, melech ha-olam asher kid'shanu b'mitzvotav v'tzivanu l'hadlik ner shel chanukah.]

Blessed is Yahweh our God, King of the universe, who performed wondrous deeds for our fathers, in olden days at this season, and has vouchsafed life and health unto us to behold the return of this festive season.

[Baruch atah Adonai eloheinu, melech ha-olam she-heh-che-oh-nu vee-kee-mo-nu ve-he-ge-o-nu liz-man ha-zeh.]

For the children of Israel, these lights remind us of the glorious events and the valiant deeds that distinguished our history during the time of the Maccabees. Antiochus Epiphanes, the king of

Syria, sought to compel Israel to give up their belief in the only true God, and to worship heathen gods.

But the members of the priestly Maccabean family arose, and gathered the faithful and pious around them. Through few in number and unaccustomed to warfare, they battled with death defying valor against the mighty and war trained Syrian armies, and Yahweh crowned their heroic efforts with victory and glory.

With praises and thanksgiving, the victors entered the Temple at Jerusalem, which the haughty enemy had defiled. They renewed its sacred rites, and appointed this Festival of Lights and Dedication. Ever sacred to us are these festive days and these symbolic lights, before which we praise Yahweh with hymns of thanksgiving for His never ending mercy and love.

For those of the Messianic Covenant, we are reminded that the Holy Anointed One of Yahweh, Yahshua, was born at Bethlehem of Judea during the Feast of Tabernacles and the temple of His body was dedicated on the eighth day of His birth.

This Festival of Lights and Dedication is a reminder that the Holy Anointed One came as a light to the world, so that whosoever believes in Him shall not perish but have everlasting life.

And this is the condemnation that light is come into the world, and men loved darkness rather than light because their deeds were evil. For everyone that does evil hates the light neither comes to the light, lest their deed should be reproved. But he that does truth comes to the light, that his deeds may be made manifest, that they are wrought in Yahweh.

We kindle these lights in remembrance of the miraculous deliverances You have wrought for Your people. These lights are sacred throughout all the eight days of Chanukah. We are to contemplate them and thus be reminded to thank and to praise You, our Father, for the wondrous miracles of our deliverance from the world and the gift of Your only begotten Son Yahshua, who has come to give us everlasting life, to all who will believe on His holy Name. We pray this in the Name of Yahshua the Messiah, Amen.

Blessed is Yahweh our God, King of the universe, who has sanctified us by His

Commandments and given us the lights of Chanukah to remind us of Your love for us.

(The Hallel is said each day of festival.)

PURIM

(Festival of Deliverance)

(Adar 14 -15)

Purim is preceded by the Fast of Esther on Adar 13 (Purim begins with the reading of the Book of Esther)

After which the following is said:

Praises and thanksgiving we offer up to Yahweh, our bountiful Father, for the paternal grace which from remotest days and in all generations You have manifested on behalf of Your people. At all times You have pleaded our cause against our enemies, and given us shelter and protection against the numberless and powerful adversaries that so frequently come against us.

If Yahweh, the faithful Guardian of Your people, had not been our aid when men stood up against us, the wicked would have destroyed us. Their hatred would have swept us away like a rapid torrent. For we were but few in number against the many enemies whose wrath raged against us. We were among the peoples of the world like a lamb among rapacious wolves and roaring lions. But You, Almighty God, have been our Rock and our Refuge in all generations. You destroyed the counsels of wickedness, and frustrated the plans which our enemies devised against us, causing them to fall into their own traps, and thereby leading the innocent and the righteous to victory.

Therefore, Yahweh our God, our hearts rejoice, and our lips give forth praises unto Your Name, and the Name of Your Holy Anointed One Yahshua. Praises be unto You Yahweh, for the innumerable wonders You have wrought in our behalf, and for the protection and assistance which You have bestowed on us to this day. In the name of Yahshua the Messiah, we pray.

B'shem Yahshua HaMashiach. Amen and Amen.

SELICHOT

(Prayer of Repentance and Fasting)

Yahweh, Master of the universe, we come to You in the Name of Yahshua the Messiah [B'Shem Yahshua Hamashiach]. Have compassion on Your children, humiliated and disgraced, torn and crushed, taken captive without cause, sold without money. We cry out in prayer and seek permission to plead before You.

Have compassion on those of us who are tortured with fetters, accustomed to blows, suffering oppression, and an object of scorn among the inhabitants of the world and a by-word among the heathen. Have compassion and see the wretchedness of Your people, listen and hear those who stand before You, who are gathered in silent supplication when chastisement comes upon us, with eyes uplifted in yearning expectation of finding Your favor.

Have compassion on those who cry out for forgiveness, who increase Your praise at all times and occasions. We join together in distress to pour forth our plea with anguished heart. Have pity, have compassion on those who have been doubly punished, devoured by the wicked, beaten and requited for numerous wrong-doings. Despite all this we have not forgotten Your Holy TORAH.

Have compassion on us as we hide our faces in shame, who bear being reviled and do not respond, as we hope for Your eternal help and trust in Your deliverance, for Your mercies have not ceased entirely, but are new every morning.

Have pity Yahweh our God. Have compassion and deliver us from our afflictions. Free our imprisonment from the land of our captivity, cure our wounds and heal our maladies, hear us when we cry and hasten the time of our redemption.

Abba Father, remember in our behalf the Messianic Covenant which You promised David Your servant, and Yahshua the Messiah, son of David and High Priest of Yahweh. Act towards us as You have promised. Bring back those who have been led astray and have mercy upon us.

Wipe away our transgressions like a thick cloud and like a mist and we will return to You for Redemption. Make our sins white as snow and wool. Sprinkle the Waters of Separation and Purification upon us and purify us, as it is written: "And I will sprinkle purifying waters upon you and you shall be pure from all your defilements and from all your idolatries I will purify you."

Have compassion on us and do not destroy us. Open our hearts to love Your Name, Yahweh and the Name of Your Holy One, Yahshua. Be accessible to us when we seek You. Bring us to Your holy mountain and make us rejoice in Your house of Prayer.

Hear our voice, Yahweh our God, and have pity and compassion upon us, and accept our prayers with mercy and favor. Bring us back to You, Yahweh, and we will return. Renew our days as of old. Do not cast us out of Your presence, and do not take Your Holy Spirit from us. Do not cast us aside in old age. Do not forsake us when our strength fails. Do not abandon us, Yahweh our God, do not keep far from us. Show us a sign of favor that our foes may see and be ashamed, because You, Yahweh, have given us aid and consoled us. Hearken to our words, Yahweh, consider our thoughts.

Do it for the sake of Your Name Yahweh, do it for the sake of Your Word, do it for the sake of Yahshua who gave His life for our Redemption, do it for the sake of Your Righteousness. Answer us when we call Abba Father, have compassion and mercy upon our cries, our torments, our sorrows and our sufferings. Hear the cry of the afflicted, the orphan, and the widow. Answer us Judge of widows, answer us Father of orphans, answer us, You who responds to the destitute and the outcast. Answer us for Your mercies sake and hear the cries of the brokenhearted, the poor and the humble in spirit.

Pardon us, our Father in Yahshua's Name, for we have sinned. Forgive us our King, for we have willfully transgressed. For You, Yahweh, are good and forgiving, and exceedingly kind to all who call upon You. Yahweh help us for the righteous are no more, for the faithful have vanished from among men. Yahweh, Lord of hosts is with us. Happy is the man who trusts in You.

Blessed is Yahweh our God, King of the universe, who hears the cry of the afflicted, the orphan, the widow, and removes fear, anxiety, and stress from our hearts.

Abba Father, I come to You in the Name of Yahshua, who died for my sins so that I might have eternal life in the Kingdom of Heaven. I open the door of my heart, I open the door of my life, and ask You to come in, to cleanse me from all sin, and to separate me from the world of sin and to remove all vestiges of pagan doctrine and tradition from my heart, from my soul. Take control of my life and make me be the kind of person You want me to be. Open my eyes, my ears, and the heart of my understanding that I may always be true to You. I ask You Father to send Your Holy Spirit to dwell in my heart and to guide me and to teach me in all things. I pray this in Yahshua's Name. Amen and Amen.

Prayer of Conversion and Baptism

The penitent convert is asked:

> Do you believe Yahshua is the Messiah the Son of Yahweh, who is Immanuel [Yahweh with us], and do you accept Him as your Savior, and invite Him into your life to be your Lord and your Master?

The penitent states:

> I do believe that Yahshua is the Messiah the Son of Yahweh, who is Immanuel, and I accept Him as my Savior. I invite Him into my life to be my Lord and my Master. Thank You Lord.

The convert is then baptized by immersion [Mikvah] in water, and the following is said:

B'Shem Yahshua HaMashiach I now baptize you for the remission of your sins. You are buried in the Waters of Purification and Separation; you are raised into a newness of life in Yahweh. You are now born-again of the Spirit; I anoint you with oil and lay my hands on you and pray that you will receive the Baptism of the Holy Spirit, with the evidence of speaking in tongues. May all the gifts of the power of the Holy Spirit be manifested in your life.

I pray in the Name of Yahshua

[B'Shem Yahshua HaMashiach]-Amen.

The Baptism of Repentance

The Prayer of Forgiveness:

In the Name of Yahshua the Messiah [B'Shem Yahshua HaMashiach] I Baptize you for the remission of your sins. I pray that you would receive the Baptism of the Holy Spirit in greater measure with the evidence of speaking in tongues. I pray that the Holy Spirit would lead you into all truth and make you obedient to the Word and the Will of Yahweh. I pray that you may have the strength and courage to remove all pagan doctrine and tradition from you mind, your soul, and your life. Amen.

(Hands are laid upon the repentant Believer and they are immersed in the Waters of Purification and instructed to never again engage in traditional practices of pagan origin. They are encouraged to keep the Commandments and Feasts of Yahweh, the Sabbaths and the Dietary Laws and to keep them with a willing heart.

Note: Those who prefer this Baptism of Repentance be done by immersion in the Waters of Purification and Separation may do so with the understanding that their sins will be remitted and they will be forgiven.)

The repentant Believer says:

> Father, forgive me for I have sinned. I have unknowingly and ignorantly engaged in religious practices which have given honor to pagan gods that are no gods. I ask Your forgiveness, and I ask that You will Baptize me with the Holy Spirit so that I may be led into all truth, and that all the gifts of the Holy Spirit may be manifested in me. In the name of Yahshua the Messiah [B'Shem Yahshua HaMashiach] I pray, Amen.

For the past two-thousand years the Church and the Children of Yahweh have engaged in many pagan religious customs and practices which is equivalent to committing spiritual adultery and fornication with pagan deities. The Baptism of Repentance is a Baptism in the Waters of Purification and Separation and a prayer of repentance for such sins is offered, whether these sins were knowingly or unknowingly committed.

Prayer of the Sick and Oppressed

When conducting a prayer for the sick and oppressed, we must always remember that the prayer is always done in the Name of Yahshua the Messiah [B'Shem Yahshua HaMashiach]. For there is no other Name in Heaven and earth given among men whereby we can be healed or receive salvation. Yahshua said that if we ask anything in His Name, He would do it. Yahshua also commanded us to heal the sick and to cast out demons in His name.

(The prayer for the sick is accompanied by a laying on of the hands upon the sick person. Initially we pray the protection of the Blood of Yahshua over us to protect us from any harm.)

"I plead the Blood of Yahshua over myself, over all who are with me, and the sick. In the Name of Yahshua the Messiah [B'Shem Yahshua HaMashiach], I command healing and deliverance from this sickness. I take authority over this sickness I bind it up and cast it into the pits of hell, never to return. I command healing in the Name of

Yahshua the Messiah [B'Shem Yahshua HaMashiach]. Thank You, Abba Father.

In casting out demons, the one who prays also pleads the Blood of Yahshua over everyone who is present. Again, the only authority we have over Satan is in the Name and by the shed Blood of Yahshua. We assert our authority and plead the protection of the shed Blood of Yahshua before we command the demons, or evil spirits to leave. Once we have established our position in Yahweh can we now command the demons to depart in the Name of Yahshua. We bind them up and cast them into the pits of hell, never to return. Then we praise Yahweh for the deliverance, singing the praises of Yahweh for all to believe in the miracles of Yahweh's love for us.

Prayer for a Family Reunion

Heavenly Father, we ask your blessing upon our family. We pray that you will provide traveling mercies upon each of us as we come to fellowship together, and may we receive the benefit of Your blessing throughout these days of sharing, these days of caring. Bless us Father as one, and may we return to bear witness of Your love for us. In Yahshua's Name we pray. Amen and Amen.

KADDISH

Prayer for The Deceased

Abba Father, full of compassion, who dwells on high, grant true rest upon the wings of the Shekinah, in the exalted spheres of the holy and pure, who shine as the resplendence of the firmament, to the soul of (__________), who has gone to his/her world, for charity has been donated in remembrance of his/her soul; may his/her place of rest be in Gad Eden. Therefore, may the all merciful One shelter him/her under the cover of His wings forever, and bind his/her soul in the bond of life. Yahweh is his/her heritage. May he/she rest in his/her resting place in peace. May his/her name be found in the Lamb's Book of Life, and let us say- Amen.

THE PASSOVER SEDER

While we refer to the parables of the Passover Seder this may seem strange to many, for who would consider the Seder as anything but a setting forth of the story of Israel's deliverance from Egypt, the suggestion is made that there is more to the story then has previously been told. Within the traditional telling of these events, there is allowed no implication other than that which is told. Perhaps in innocence there is assumed to be nothing more.

The questions were never asked because esoteric implications were never envisioned. While we "enlightened ones" might scoff at such an idea, it must be brought out that, other than proclaiming that the Messiah is the Passover Lamb, most of us don't have the faintest idea as to what a Passover Seder is. Our enlightenment therefore seems to reflect our own lack of understanding as well.

Whatever the case, for we all lack knowledge about most things, therefore we can easily forgive one another for lacking knowledge about this as well. It is our purpose to explore esoteric implication inherent in the ritual of the Seder. Naturally, as believers in Yahshua as the Messiah, our interpretations, and renderings will be biased towards foundational truth.

With this in mind Yahweh will guide us by His Spirit to bring forth a telling of Yahweh's magnificent deliverance available to all who seek to escape the bondage of this world. The "Promised Land" is within our grasp. Let us go forth to receive that which Yahweh has prepared for us.

Briefly, before I go on I must tell you the blessing I have received as I have prepared this script for your use. The final telling of Israel's redemption is about to take place in the full knowledge that Yahshua is the Lamb of Yahweh who takes away the sins of the world. My praise and thanks to the Holy Spirit who has used me in this capacity to reveal the secret treasures of our Father's testimony of His Son, Yahshua.

The commandment to institute the Passover was given to Moses with instructions concerning how it was to be observed at the time Yahweh passed through the land of Egypt to destroy the first-born of all, both men and beasts. It is the tenth plague Yahweh put on the Egyptians and it was the decisive one as far as forcing Pharaoh to allow the children of Yahweh to depart from slavery and bondage.

The telling of this story of redemption and deliverance is an annual reminder of what Yahweh did for the children of Israel, and what He does for us even today. The implication being that in every generation we too are delivered from slavery and more specific is the reminder that we as slaves held bondage by the world are also called upon to leave the things of the world and to take the path through the cloud and the sea and to enter into the promised land of Yahweh's blessings. That there are "giants in the land" is of no consequence, for Yahweh is able to deliver us from bondage, and from those who would oppress us.

In commemoration of this deliverance Yahweh has set forth an excellent object lesson in the form of the Passover Seder. To remind us, of not only the deliverance of Israel from Egyptian bondage, but also the deliverance He has given each of us through His Son Yahshua. Without going into detail at this time we set forth the items which serve as visual aids to this greatest of all object lessons.

Three Matzah known as the Bread of Affliction, are placed upon a plate before us and covered. The middle Matzah which is broken and given for us, was hidden (buried) and then resurrected with the promise of Aphikomon (the Messiah has come and is coming again).

The roasted shank bone of a lamb represents the Passover Lamb. Moror-horseradish (a bitter herb) Haroses (a mixture of apples, blanched almonds, and raisins finely chopped and flavored with grape juice).

Parsley

Salt Water

Wine (Grape juice)

A roasted egg

Several items not present in a modern Passover Seder is the Lamb, the Blood, and the Hyssop. The lamb we know as a sacrifice, the blood a covering, the hyssop a cleansing, and the sprinkling of the blood with the hyssop was symbolic of purification. "Purge me with hyssop, and I shall be clean: wash me and I shall be whiter than snow."

SETTING THE TABLE

On the table in front of the head of the house, or leader of the Seder, set a large platter upon which is placed the following:

A Shank Bone

One Egg

Some Horseradish (Bitter Herb)

Some Parsley (Celery)

Some Haroseth

Beside the platter place three Matzah each of which is covered separately in the folds of a napkin or special cover. For use by the others at the table place:

A plate of Horseradish cut into small pieces.

A dish of Haroseth

Some Parsley (or Celery)

A dish of Salt Water, and

A cup of Grape juice is placed at each plate, and

In the center of the table place a cup for the Prophet Elijah. This is traditionally called the Cup of Elijah.

Hebrew tradition holds reference to the custom of reclining on the left side during the meal, a position assumed by free men. However, Scripture tells us that the first Passover Seder was eaten with loins girded, shoes on the feet, staff in hand, and the meal should be eaten in haste. Other than the fact that the Israelites were about to leave Egypt shortly after eating the meal the object lesson here is to show how quickly Yahweh wants us to depart from our worldly ways.

That is, immediately after receiving Him as Lord of our lives. Yahweh knows the danger of our loitering in the pits of corruption. He therefore commands us to depart quickly before the fires of hell consume us and before the cares of the world choke out the Word of Yahweh received in our hearts.

The table is usually spread with the best of the family's china and silverware, and adorned with flowers in keeping with the festive spirit.

THE ORDER OF THE SEDER SERVICE

1. Recite the sanctification of the festival.

2. Partake of the parsley dipped in salt water.

3. Break the middle matzos, and hide half of it to be eaten at the end of the meal.

4. Recite the story of Israel's deliverance and give testimony of personal salvation.

5. Wash the Hands.

6. Bless the meal and the matzo.

7. Combine the matzo, bitter herbs, and the Haroseth, and eat them together.

8. Eat the festive meal.

9. End the meal by eating the Aphikomon.

10. Say Grace.

I l. Recite the Hallel.

12. End with Prayer for the acceptance of the service.

LIGHTING THE FESTIVAL LIGHTS

To symbolize the joy which the festival brings into the home, the wife, with her head covered, kindles the lights while the Leader of the Seder says:

> Yahshua said, "I am come a light into the world, that whosoever believeth on me should not abide in darkness."

The wife now recites the following blessing:

> Blessed is Yahweh our God, King of the universe, who has sanctified us by His commandments, and has commanded us to kindle the festival lights.

The Leader says:

> Blessed is Yahweh our God, King of the universe, who has kept us alive and sustained us and brought us to this season. May our home be consecrated Abba Father by the light of Your countenance, shining upon us in

blessing, and bringing us peace! In the name of Yahshua we pray, Amen.

The Leader lifts up the cup and says:

Let us praise Yahweh and thank Him for all the blessings He has given us; for life, health and strength; for home, love and friendship, for the discipline of our trails, and temptations; for the happiness of our success and prosperity.

In love You have given us, Yahweh our God, solemn days of joy, and festive seasons of gladness, even this day of the Feast of the Passover, a holy convocation, a memorial of our departure from bondage, and of Your Son Yahshua the Messiah. You have chosen us for Your service and have made us coheirs with Yahshua in the blessings of Your holy festivals. Blessed are You Abba Father who sanctifies Israel and the festive seasons. In Yahshua's name we pray-Amen.

All in unison say:

> Blessed is Yahweh our God, King of the universe, who creates the fruit of the vine.

DRINK THE FIRST CUP

The Leader now reads:

> Yahshua said, “you have not chosen me, but I have chosen you, and ordained you, that you should go and bring forth fruit, and that your fruit should remain: that whatsoever you shall ask of the Father in my name, He may give it you.”

PARTAKE OF THE PARSLY

Some Parsley is distributed to all present who dip it in salt water, and before eating it the Leader reads:

> “Who hath believed our report? To whom is the arm of Yahweh revealed? For he shall grow up before him as a tender plant, and as a root out of a dry ground: He hath neither form nor comeliness; and when we shall see him there is no beauty that we should desire him.
>
> He is despised and rejected of men; a man of sorrows, and acquainted with grief: and we hid as it were our faces from him; he was despised, and we esteemed him not.” Yahshua said, “I am the true vine, and my Father is the husbandman. Every branch in me that bears not fruit He takes away: and every branch that bears fruit, he purges it; that it may bring forth more fruit.”

All say in unison:

> Blessed is Yahweh our God, King of the universe, creator of the fruit of the earth.

BREAK THE MIDDLE MATZO

The Leader of the Seder breaks the middle matzo, leaving one half on the dish, and hides the other half as the Aphikomon is to be eaten at the end of the meal. The Leader lifts up the plate of matzo and says:

This is the Bread of Affliction which our fathers ate in the land of Egypt. Let all who are hungry come and eat. Let all who are in want come and celebrate the Passover with us. May it be Yahweh's will to redeem us from all trouble and from all servitude? Next year at this season, may the whole house of Israel be free.

"Surely he has born our grief, and carried our sorrows: yet we did esteem him stricken, smitten of Yahweh and afflicted. But he was wounded for our transgressions; he was bruised for our iniquities: the chastisement of our peace was upon him; and with his stripes we are healed."

The Leader now replaces the Matzah plate upon the table.

THE FOUR QUESTIONS

The youngest person at the table asks:

1. Why is this night different from all other nights? On all other nights, we eat either leavened or unleavened bread. Why, on this night do we eat only unleavened bread?

2. On all other nights, we eat all kinds of herbs. Why, on this night do we eat especially bitter herbs?

3. On all other nights, we do not dip herbs in any condiment. Why, on this night, do we dip them in salt water and Haroseth?

4. On other nights, we eat without special festivities. Why, on this night, do we hold this Seder Service?

The Leader answers:

We celebrate tonight because we were Pharaoh's bondmen in Egypt and Yahweh our God delivered us with a mighty hand. Had not Yahweh redeemed us from Egypt, we, our children, and our children's children would have remained slaves. It is our duty from year to year, to tell the story of the deliverance from Egypt and our deliverance from the bondage of the world.

THE FOUR SONS

The Leader says:

To the wise son you say:

> "This service is held in order to worship Yahweh our God that it may be well with us all the days of our lives."

To the wicked son you say:

> "It is because of that which Yahweh did for me when I came forth out of Egypt and was delivered from the bondage of this world."

To the simple son you say:

> "By strength of hand Yahweh brought us out of Egypt, and out of the house of bondage."

For the son who is unable to ask, you shall explain the whole story of Passover: "And you shall tell your son in that day, saying:

"It is because of that which Yahweh did for me when I came forth out of Egypt".

STORY OF THE OPPRESSION

It is well for all of us whether young or old to consider how Yahweh's help has been our unfailing stay and support through times of trial and persecution. Ever since He called Abraham from the bondage of idolatry to His service of truth, He has been our Guardian; for not in one country alone, nor in one age have violent men risen up against the children of Yahweh, but in every generation and in every land, tyrants have sought to destroy us; and Yahweh has delivered us from their hands.

The Scriptures tell us that Jacob went down into Egypt, and sojourned there, few in number. Joseph preceded his brethren and Jacob his father into the land of Egypt and was governor over the all the land of Egypt. The children of Israel dwelt in the land of Goshen. They were fruitful, and multiplied exceedingly.

When Jacob, Joseph and his brothers died there arose a new ruler over Egypt, who knew not Joseph. And he said, "Behold, the people of Israel are too many and too mighty for us; come let us deal wisely with them lest they multiply, and bring harm upon us. Therefore they set over them task masters to afflict them with burdens. But the more the Egyptians afflicted them the more the Israelites multiplied.

The Egyptians dealt evil upon the children of Israel and made them suffer. They set upon them hard work, and made the children labor rigorously. We cried unto Yahweh, the God of our fathers, and Yahweh heard our cries and saw our affliction, our toil and our oppression. And Yahweh brought us forth out of Egypt, with a mighty hand, with an outstretched arm, with great terror, with signs and with wonders.

By Himself, in His Glory, Yahweh passed through the land of Egypt on that fateful night, and smote all the first-born in the land of Egypt from man to beasts, and against all the gods of Egypt He executed His judgments.

He sent Moses and Aaron and He brought forth His people with joy, His chosen ones with singing. He guided them in the wilderness, as a shepherd his flock. Therefore He commanded that we are to observe the Passover in its season, from year to year, throughout all our generations; that His law shall be in our mouths and that we shall declare His might unto our children and our children's children His salvation throughout all our generations.

Yahshua said: I am the Good Shepherd, and know my sheep, and am known of mine. As the Father knows me, even so know I the Father: and I lay down my lift for the sheep. And other sheep I have, which are not of this fold: them also I must bring, and they shall hear my voice; and there shall be one fold, and one shepherd. Therefore does the Father love me, because I lay down my life, that I might take it again? No man takes it from me, but I lay it down, and I have power to take it again. This commandment have I received of my Father.

All read in unison:

Who is like You, Abba Yahweh, among the mighty? Who is like You glorious in holiness, fearful in praises, doing wonders? Yahweh shall reign forever and ever. How much more are we to be grateful to Yahweh our God, for the manifold favors which He has bestowed upon us.

Yahweh brought us out of Egypt and bondage, divided the Red Sea, permitted us to cross on dry land, sustained us for forty years in the desert, fed us with manna, ordained the Sabbath, brought us to Mount Sinai, gave us the Scriptures, led us into the land of promise, built for us the Tabernacle, sent unto us prophets of truth, made us a holy people and given us the Feasts as a memorial to Your Son Yahshua.

The Leader of the Seder says:

At this point it is good for each of us to remember what Yahweh has done for us. Let each of us remember and tell our story of how we were personally delivered from bondage and how Yahshua has delivered us from bondage to the world and set us free.

"For Yahweh so loved the world that He gave His only begotten Son, that whosoever believes in him shall not perish but have everlasting life."

THE PASSOVER SYMBOLS

The Leader says:

Should our enemies ever assail us, the reminder of the exodus from Egypt and our exodus from worldly bondage will never fail to inspire us with new courage, and the symbols of this festival will help to strengthen our faith in Yahweh our God and Yahshua the Messiah, who redeems us from oppression.

Someone asks:

What is the meaning of the Passover Lamb? The Leader lifts up the roasted shank-bone and answers:

The Passover Lamb, as represented by this roasted shank-bone, was eaten as a memorial of Yahweh's favor, as it is said: "It is the sacrifice of Yahweh's Passover, for that He passed over the houses of the children of Israel in Egypt when He smote the Egyptians and delivered our houses". As Yahweh passed over and spared the houses of Israel, so did He save us, by His Son Yahshua, from all kinds of distress, and so may He always shield the afflicted, and for evermore remove every trace of bondage from among the children of man.

The Passover Lamb is the one-time sacrifice Yahshua made for our sins. He is the Savior of the world. "He was oppressed, and He was afflicted, yet He opened not His mouth: He was brought as a lamb to the slaughter, and as a sheep before her shearers is dumb, so He opened not His mouth."

And one of the elders saith unto me, Weep not" behold the Lion of the tribe of Judah, the Root of David, hath prevailed to open the book, and to lose the seven seals thereof. And I beheld, and, in the midst of the throne and of the four beasts, and in the midst of the elders, stood a Lamb as it had been slain, having seven horns and seven eyes.

These are the seven Spirits of Yahweh sent forth into all the earth. And He came and took the book out of the right hand of Him that sat upon the throne. And when He had taken the book, the four beasts and four and twenty elders fell down before the Lamb, having every one of them harps, and golden vials full of odors, which are the prayers of the saints. And they sang a new song, saying,

"You are worthy to take the book, and to open the seals thereof: For you were slain, and have redeemed us to Yahweh by your Blood out of every kindred, and tongue, and people and nation; and have made us unto Yahweh, Kings and priests and we shall reign on the earth." And I beheld, and I heard the voice of many angels round about the throne and the beasts and the elders: and the number of them was ten thousand times ten thousand and thousands of thousands; saying with a loud voice, 'Worthy is the Lamb that was slain to receive power, and riches and wisdom, and strength, and honor, and glory, and blessing."

Someone asks:

What is the meaning of the Matzah?

The Leader lifts up the Matzah and answers:

Matzah, which is called the Bread of Affliction was baked without leaven and represented the affliction of the children of Israel in Egypt. It also portrays the physical suffering of Yahshua when He was sacrificed upon the tree the altar of His Love for us.

As the Psalmist says, "Be not far from me; for trouble is near; for there is none to help.

Many bulls have compassed me: strong bulls of Bashan have beset me round. They gaped upon me with their mouths, as a ravening and a roaring lion. I am poured out like water, and all my bones are out of joint: my heart is like wax; it is melted in the midst of my bowels. My strength is dried up like a potsherd; and my tongue cleaves to my jaws; and You have brought me into the dust of death. For dogs have compassed me: the assembly of the wicked has enclosed me: they pierced my hands and my feet. I may tell all my bones: they look and stare at me. They part my garments among them, and cast lots upon my vesture."

Someone asks:

And what is the meaning of the bitter herbs?

The Leader lifts the bitter and answers:

We eat the bitter herb to recall the lives of our ancestors who were embittered by the

Egyptians: “And they made their lives bitter with hard labor in mortar and bricks and in all manner of field labor. Whatever task was imposed upon them was executed with the utmost rigor.” As we eat the bitter herbs in the midst of the festivities of this night, we rejoice in the trials which have strengthened us. Instead of becoming embittered by them, we were sustained and strengthened.

In every generation we must look upon ourselves as if we personally had come out of Egypt. It is because of that which Yahweh did for me when I came forth from the bondage of the world. It was not only our forefathers whom Yahweh has redeemed; he has redeemed us as well.

“Yet it pleased Yahweh to bruise Him, He has put Him to grief; when He made His soul an offering for sin, Yahweh shall prosper His days, and the pleasure of Yahweh shall prosper in His hand. He shall see the travail of His soul, and shall be satisfied: by His knowledge shall my righteous servant justify many; for He shall bear their iniquities. Therefore will I divide him a portion for the great, and he shall divide the spoil with the strong; because he hath poured out his soul unto death. He was numbered with the transgressors; and he bares the sin of many, and makes intercession for the transgressors."

All say in unison:

Therefore it is our duty to thank and to praise in song and prayer, to glory and extol Him who performed all these wonders for our forefathers and for us. He brought us from slavery to freedom, from anguish to joy, from sorrow to festivity, from darkness to great light. Let us therefore sing before Him a new song.

Blessed is the Name of Yahweh.

The cups are filled for the second time. Raising the cups all read in unison:

"Blessed is Yahweh our God, King of the universe, who creates the fruit of the vine."

DRINK THE SECOND CUP

The upper Matzah is broken and distributed.

All then read in unison:

> "Blessed is Yahweh our God, King of the universe, who brings forth bread from the earth. "Blessed is Yahweh our God, King of the universe, who hast sanctified us through His commandments, and ordained that we should eat unleavened bread. "

The Leader then reads:

> The cup of blessing which we bless, is it not the communion of the Blood of the Messiah? The bread which we break, is it not the

communion of the Body of the Messiah? For we being many are one bread, and one body: for we are all partakers of that one bread."

WASH THE HANDS

The Leader reads:

Yahshua knowing that our Father had given all things into his hands, and that he was come from Yahweh, and went to Yahweh; He rose from supper, laid aside his garments, took a towel, and girded himself. After that he poured water into a basin, and began to wash the disciples' feet, and to wipe them with the towel wherewith he was girded.

After he had washed their feet, and had taken his garments, and was set down again, he said unto them, "Do you know what I have done to you? You call me Master and Lord: and you say well; for so I am. If I then, your Lord and

> Master, have washed your fleet; so also should you wash one another's feet. I have given you an example that you should do as I have done to you."

The Leader then washes his hands and says:

> Blessed is Yahweh our God, King of the universe, who hast sanctified us by His commandments, and commanded us concerning the washing of the hands and the feet.

BLESSING OF THE MEAL

Each person receives some bitter herbs and Haroseth, which he places between two pieces of Matzah.

The Leader then reads:

The combination of unleavened bread and the bitter herbs and the eating of them together are to carry out the injunction concerning the Passover sacrifice:

"With unleavened bread and with bitter herbs, they shall eat it."

All read in unison:

"Blessed is Yahweh our God, King of the universe, who hast sanctified us by His commandments, and ordained that we should eat bitter herbs.

Everyone now eats the combination.

PASSOVER SUPPER IS NOW SERVED

PARTAKE OF THE APHIKOMON

At the conclusion of the meal the head of the house redeems the Aphikomon and distributes pieces of it to all present, and then reads:

> "For I have received of Yahweh that also I delivered unto you that Yahshua the same night in which He was betrayed took bread: And when He had given thanks, He brake it, and said, "Take, eat: this is my body, which is broken for you, do this in remembrance of me."

All say in unison:

> "Blessed is Yahweh our God, King of the universe, who brings forth bread from the earth.

EAT THE APHIKOMON

The cups are filled for the Third time.

The Leader reads:

> After the same manner he took the cup, and when he had supped, he said, "This cup is the new testament in my blood: Do this as often as you drink it in remembrance of me. For as often as you eat this bread and drink this cup you show Yahshua's death till he comes."

All say in unison:

> "Blessed is Yahweh our God, King of the universe, who creates the fruit of the vine.

DRINK THE THIRD CUP

The door is opened for Elijah. All rise.

The Leader reads:

> Behold, I will send you Elijah the prophet before the coming of the great and dreadful day of Yahweh: And he shall turn the heart of the fathers to the children, and the heart of the children to their fathers, lest I come and smite the earth with a curse.

The door is closed. All are seated.

The cups are filled for the Fourth time.

The Leader lifts the cup and reads:

> The festive service is now completed. With songs of praise, we have lifted the cups symbolizing the divine promises of salvation, and have called upon the name of Yahweh.

> As we offer the benediction over the fourth cup, let us again lift our souls to Yahweh in

faith believing on His Son Yahshua. May He who broke Pharaoh's yoke forever shatter all fetters of oppression, and hasten the day when swords shall, at last, be broken and wars cease. May the glad tidings of redemption be heard in all lands? May Yahweh bless the whole house of Israel with freedom, and keep us safe from danger everywhere. May Yahweh cause the light of His countenance to shine upon all men, and dispel the darkness of ignorance and prejudice.

May Yahweh lift up His countenance upon our country and render it a true home of liberty and a bulwark of justice. May Yahweh grant peace unto the house of Israel, unto us and unto all mankind. In Yahshua's Name we pray-Amen and Amen.

All say in unison:

"Blessed is Yahweh our God, King of the universe, who creates the land and the fruit of the vine.

DRINK THE FOURTH CUP

The Leader says:

> The Seder is ended. As Yahshua said when He died for us, "It is finished."

Everyone says in unison:

NEXT YEAR IN JERUSALEM!

HEBREW BLESSINGS

(English with Hebrew transliterations)

THY FAITHFULNESS IS GREAT

Blessed is Yahweh our God, King of the universe. I offer thanks to You living and eternal King, for You have mercifully restored my soul within me. Your faithfulness is great.

[Baruch atah Adonai eloheinu, melech ha-Olam modeh ani L'fonecha, melech chai v'kayom, she-heche-zarto bi nishmosi b'chemlo raboh emunosecho.]

BLESSING OF THE WASHING OF THE HANDS

Blessed is Yahweh our God, King of the universe, who has sanctified us with His commandments, and commanded us concerning the washing of the hands.

[Baruch atah Adonai eloheinu, melech ha-Olam Asher kid'shanu b'mitzvotav v'tzivanu al n'tilas yadayim.]

THE PRIESTLY BENEDICTION

May Yahweh bless you and keep you. May Yahweh make His countenance shine upon you and be gracious to you. May Yahweh turn His countenance towards you and grant you peace.

[Y'varekh'kha Adonai v'yishm'rekha ya'er Adonai panau elekha vihuneka yisa Adonai panau elekha v'yasem lecha shalom.]

HEAR, O ISRAEL-(SHEMA)

Hear, O Israel, Yahweh is our God, Yahweh is One. Blessed is His Name, and His glorious Kingdom forever and ever.

[Shema yisra-ayl Adonai eloheinu Adonai echad. Baruch shem k'vod mal'chuso l'olam va-ed]

LIGHTING THE CANDLES

Blessed is Yahweh our God, King of the universe, who has sanctified us with His commandments, and commanded us to kindle the light of the Holy Sabbath.

[Baruch atah Adonai eloheinu, melech ha-olam asher kid'shanu b'mitzvotav v'tzivanu l'hadlik ner shel Shabbat kodesh.]

BLESSING OF THE BREAD

Blessed is Yahweh our God, King of the universe, who brings forth bread from the earth.

[Baruch atah Adonai eloheinu, melech ha-olam ha-motsea l'kim min ha-aretz]

BLESSING OF THE WINE (Grape Juice)

Blessed is Yahweh our God, King of the universe, who creates the fruit of the vine.

[Baruch atah Adonai eloheinu, melech ha-olam borei prei ha-gafen.]

BLESSING OF THE VARIOUS SPICES

Blessed is Yahweh our God, King of the universe, who creates the various kinds of spices.

[Baruch atah Adonai eloheinu, melech ha-olam borei minei besamim.]

BLESSING OF THE HAVDALAH LIGHT

Blessed is Yahweh our God, King of the universe who has sanctified us by His commandments and has commanded us to kindle the Havdalah lights.

[Baruch atah Adonai eloheinu, melech ha-olam asher kid'shanu b'mitzvotav v'tzivanu l'hadlik ner shel Havdalah.]

BLESSING FOR REACHING A FESTIVAL SEASON

Blessed is Yahweh our God, King of the universe, who has kept us alive, sustained us and brought us to this festive season.

[Baruch atah Adonai eloheinu, melech ha-olam she-heh-che-yoh-nu vee-kee-mo-nu ve-he-ge-onu liz-man ha-zeh.]

BLESSING FOR THE EVE OF A FESTIVAL

Blessed is Yahweh our God, King of the universe, who has sanctified us with His commandments, and has commanded us to kindle the lights of the festival.

[Baruch atah Adonai eloheinu, melech ha-olam, asher kid'shanu b'mitzvotav v'tzivanu l'hadlik ner shel Yom Tov.]

BLESSING FOR THE MIRACLES OF THE FESTIVAL SEASON

Blessed is Yahweh our God, King of the universe who has performed wondrous deeds for our fathers in olden days, at this season, and for us in times past.

[Baruch atah Adonai eloheinu melech ha-olam ner shel she-bus ve-shel Yom Tov.]

BLESSING OF THE LULAV

Blessed is Yahweh our God, King of the universe, who has sanctified us with His commandments, and has commanded us concerning the taking of the palm branch.

[Baruch atah Adonai eloheinu, melech ha-olam asher kid'shanu b'mitzvotav v'tzivanu al ne-tee-las Lulav.]

BLESSED IS YOUR NAME

Blessed is Your Name and your glorious Kingdom forever and ever.

[Baruch shem k'vod mal'chuso l'olam va-ed.]

BLESSED IS YAHWEH

Blessed is Yahweh. Blessed is Yahweh forever and ever.

[Baruch atah Adonai-- Baruch atah Adonai l'olam va-ed.]

LOVE YAHWEH YOUR GOD

You shall love Yahweh your God with all your heart, with all your soul and with all your might. And these words which I command you today shall be upon your heart. You shall teach them diligently to your children, and you shall speak of them when you walk on the road, when you lie down and when you rise. You shall bind them as a sign upon your hand, and they shall be as frontlets between your eyes, and you shall write them upon the doorposts of your house and upon your gates.

WEEKLY TORAH READINGS

GENESIS

Bereshith	1:1-6:18
Noah	6:19-11:32
Lekh Lekha	12:1-17
VaYera	18:1-22
Chayay Sarah	23:1-25:18
Toledoth	25:19-28:9
VaYetze	28:10-32:3
VaYishlach	32:4-36
VaYeshev	37:1-40
Miketz	41:1-44:17
VaYigash	44:18-47:27
VaYechi	47:28-49

EXODUS

Shemoth	1:1-6:1
VaEra	6:2-9
Bo	10:1-13:16
Beshalach	13:17-17
Yithro	18:1-20
Mishpatim	21:1-24
Terumah	25:1-27:19
Tetzaveh	27:20-30:10
Ki Thisa	30:11-34
VaYakhel	35:1-38:20
Pekudey	38:21-40

LEVITICUS

VaYikra	1:1-5
Tzav	6:1-8
Shemini	9:1-11
Tazria	12:1-13
Metzorah	14:1-15
Acharey Moth	16:1-18
Kedoshim	19:1-20
Emor	21:1-24
Behar	25:1-26:2
BeChuko-Thai	26:3-27

NUMBERS

BeMidbar	1:1-4:20
Naso	4:21-7
BeHa'Alothekha	8:1-12
Sh'lach	13:1-15
Korach	16:1-18
Chukath	19:1-22:1
Balak	22:2-25:9
Pinchas	25:10-30:1
Mattoth	30:2-32
Massey	33:1-36

DEUTERONOMY

Devarim	1:1-3:22
VeEthChanan	3:23-7:11
Ekev	7:12-11:25
Re'eh	11:26-16:17
Shof'tim	16:18-21:9
Ki Thetze	21:10-25
Ki Thavo	26:1-29:8
Netzavim	29:9-30
VaYelekh	31:1-31
HaAzinu	32:1-32
VeZoth HaBerakhah	33:1-34

TORAH/TENACH READINGS FOR THE FESTIVALS

ROSH CHODESH - Head of the Month - Num. 28:1-15

SABBATH ROSH CHODESH - Num. 28:1-15; Isa. 66:1-24

ROSH HASHANAH - Head of the Year - Tishrei 1

1st day: Gen. 21; I Sam. 1:1-20

2nd day: Gen. 22; Jer. 31:1-19

FAST OF GEDALIAH - Tishrei 3 - Ex. 32:11-14; 34:1-10; Isa. 55:6-56:8

YOM KIPPUR - Tishrei 10

Morning Prayer (Shacharit) Lev. 16; Isa. 57:14-58:14

Afternoon Prayer (Minchah) Lev. 18; Book of Jonah

SUCCOS - Tishrei 15-23

Tishrei 15 - First day - Lev. 22:26-23:44; Zech. 14:1-21; Matt. 1:18-22; Luke 1:26-38

Tishrei 16 - Second day - Lev. 22:26-23:44; I Kings 8:2-22; Luke 2:1-20

Tishrei 17 - Third day - Num. 29:17-25; Matt. 2:1-12 (Chol Hamoed - Day 1)

Tishrei 18 - Fourth day - Num. 29:20-28;

Tishrei 19 - Malachi 4:2-5; Matt. 2:13-18 (Chol Hamoed - Day 2)

Tishrei 20 - Fifth day - Num. 29:23-31; Luke 1:5-25 (Chol Hamoed - Day 3)

Tishrei 21 - Sixth day - Num. 29:26-34; Matt. 3:1-3 (Chol Hamoed - Day 4)

Sabbath - Ex. 33:12-34:26 (Chol Hamoed)

HOSHANA RABBAH - Num. 29:26-34; John 1:1-14

SHEMINI ATZERES - Deut. 14:22-16:17; I Kings 8:54-9:1

SIMCHAS TORAH - Gen. 1:1-2:3; Deut. 33:1-34:12; Jos. 1:1-81; Luke 2:21-40

CHANUKAH - Kislev 25 - Tevet 2

Kislev 25 - Num. 7:1-17

Kislev 26 - Num. 7:18-29

Kislev 27 - Num. 7:24-35

Kislev 28 - Num. 7:30-41

Kislev 29 - Num. 7:36-47

Kislev 30 - Num. 7:48-59; 28:1-15

(Rosh Chodesh)

Tevet 1 - Num. 7:48-59; 28:1-15

(Rosh Chodesh)

Tevet 2 – Ezek. 45:16 – 46:18

First Sabbath - Zech. 2:14-4:7

Second Sabbath - I Kings 7:40-50

Sabbath immediately preceding Rosh Chodesh – I Sam. 20:18-42

TENTH OF TEVET - Tevet 10 - Ex. 32:11-14; 34:1-10; Isa. 55:6-56:8

FAST OF ESTHER - Adar 13 - Ex. 32:11-14; 34:1-10; Isa. 55:6-56:8

PURIM - Adar 14-15 - Ex. 17:8-16, Book of Esther

PASSOVER - Nisan 14-21

Nisan 14 – First Passover Seder
Ex. 12:21-51; Lev. 23: 5; Jos. 3:5-7, 5:2, 6:1, 27; Luke 22:47-53, 23:1-54.

Nisan 15 – Second Passover Seder
Lev. 23:6-8; II Kings 23:1-9, 21-25; John 18:1-19:42

Sabbath during the intermediate days of Passover - Exod. 33:12 – 34:26; Num. 28:19-25.

Nisan 16 – Chol Hamoed – Day 1

Ex. 13:1-16; Lev. 23:10-14; John 20:1-10; I Cor. 5:20-23

Nisan 17 – Chol Hamoed – Day 2

Ex. 22:24-23:19; Lev. 23:15.

Nisan 18 – Chol Hamoed – Day 3

Ex. 34:1-26; Nu. 28:19-25.

Nisan 19 - Chol Hamoed – Day 4
Num. 9:1-14, 28:19-25.

Nisan 20 - Seventh Day
Num.33:12-34:26; Ezek. 37:1-4 Ex. 13:17-15:26; II Sam. 22:1-51.

Nisan 21 – Eighth Day

Deut. 14:22, 15:19-16:17; Isa. 10:32-12:6.

SHAVUOS - Sivan 6-Ex. 19:1-20:23; Lev. 23:15-22; Ezek. 1:1-28, 3:12; Acts 2:1-39

SEVENTEENTH OF TAMMUZ - Tammuz 17
Ex. 32:11-14, 34:1-10; Isa. 55:6-56:8

TISH B'AV - Av 9

Morning Prayer (Shacharit) Deut. 4:25-40; Jer. 8:13-9:23

Afternoon Prayer (Minchah) Ex. 32:11-14; 34:1-10; Isa. 55:6-56:8

SCRIPTURE FOR EMOTIONAL NEEDS

ABANDONMENT - Ezra 10:3

ABUSE - Gen.16:9; Exod.20:4-5; Isa.50:4-6

ADDICTION - Prov.5:22-23; Jer.13:23; Mark 9:43-47

ADULTERY - Gen. 35:22; Num.5:31; Prov.2:22, 5:3-10, 22-23, 23:27, 31:3; Ezek. 23:25; Matt. 19:1-9; Mark 10:1-2

ALCOHOL - Gen.9:22-25; Lev.l0:9; Psalms104:14-15; 116:13; Prov.20:1, 23:29-35; Luke1:15; John 2:1-11; I Tim.5:23

AMBITION - Gen.11:4; Num.16:3; Judg.18:20; Jer.45:5; Matt.20:20-21; I Cor. 7:17, 20, 26

ANGER - I Chr.13:11; Job 15:13, 32-2-5, 19; Prov.14:29; Dan.2:5; Acts 15:39; Eph.4:26; James 1:19-20

ANXIETY - Matt.6:25-34; Luke12:22-34; Phil.4:4-9

ARGUMENTS - Job 18:2; Acts 15:39

ASSURANCE - Ps.37; Romans 8; II Tim.1:8-12; I John 2:28, 3:24, 5:9-13

ATONEMENT - Isa.27:8-9, 53:5; Ezek.16:63; John 1:29; Rom.3:25

ATTITUDE - Gen. 4:8-7; Ps. 73:3, 77:12, 81:11, 86:11; Eccl. 11:10; Isa. 1:11-14; Jer.17:10; Joel 2:113; Phil.4:8; Col.3:2

BETRAYAL - Ps. 41:9, 109:1-3; Jer. 40:16, 41:6; Obad.7; Matt 26:14-16, 49, 75; Mark 14:10, 45, 72; Luke 22:47, 61-62

BITTERNESS - Ruth 1:13, 20-21; Job 15:13, 38:2; Ps. 140:10

BLAME - Gen.16:5; Judg.19, 25, 20:6; I Kings 17:18, 20; Hosea 4:4

BLASPHEMY - Exod.20:7; Lev.24:13-23; Matt.9:1-8, 26:57-67; Mark 3:20-30

BRIBES - Prov.17:8, 21:14, 22:16

CLEANNESS - Lev. 11-15; Num.19; Ps. 51:1-9; Heb.10:19-22; I John 1:5-10

COMPORT - Job 4:1; Ps. 23:4; Chr.1:5

COMMITMENT - Gen.15:6; Deut. 33:9; Ruth 1:16-18; Ps. 31:15, 40:6, 86:11; Prov. 23:15; Isa.

58:6-7; Jer.9:2, 26:10-16; Ezek.20:3; Zech.13:3; Luke 4:26; John 6:51, 53-58; II Tim.3:7; Rev.3:16

COMPASSION - Prov. 24:11; Isa. 21:3-4; Jer. 4:19-26, 48:31-32, 36; Mark 2:4; Luke 5:19; Gal.6:2, 5

COMPLAINING - Exod.16:7, 17:2; Num.21:5-6; Job 6:5; Ps.3:1; Eccl.5:19-20; Isa. 45:9; Jer. 45:3

CONFESSION - Josh.7:19; II Sam, 12:13; Num.1:6; Job 16:17; Prov.14:9, 28:13; John 9:41; I John 1:9

CONSCIENCE - Gen.39:9; Deut.28:65; Josh.1:1; Job 13:25; Ps.19:13; Prov.20:27; Ezek.38:22-23; Acts 24:25; Rom.14:13, 22-23; I Cor. 8:10-11

CONTENTMENT - Ps.23:1; Eccl.1:6-8; I Cor.7:17, 20, 26; I Tim.6:6-8

COURAGE - Josh.1:9; I Sam.17:26-50; Dan.3; Acts 4, 5:17-42

COVETING - Exod. 20:17; Josh. 7; I Kings 21:1-14; James 4:1-10

CRITICISM - Job 6:15-17; Ps.64:3-6; Prov.12:1, 27:6, 29:19; Eccl.10:20; Jer.18:19-23; Rom.14:4

DEBTS - Exod. 21:2; Deut. 15:1; Neh. 5:5; Prov. 22:7; Matt. 18:24-28

DECEPTION - II Sam. 13:6, 16:4; II Chr. 18:29; Jer. 41:6

DEDICATION - Lev. 27:2, 27:26-29; Neh. 12:27-43

DEMON POSSESSION - Matt. 8:28-34; Mark 1:23, 5:1-10; Luke 4:33; Acts 16:16-19; I Tim.4:1-10

DENIAL - Ps.32:3; Ezek. 33:32; Mark 16:7

DEPRESSION - Job 17:15; Ps.63:1-3; Prov. 25:20; Eccl. 4:1- 3

DESPAIR - I Kings 11:10-12; Job7:8-10, 15-16, 7:22.24; Ps. 10:1, 142:6; Eccl. 1:15; Isa. 33:7-9; Jer. 8:20; Ezek.37:11

DISCIPLINE - Ps.6:1, 66:10, 94:12-13, 141:5; Prov. 3:1-12, 19:18; Jer. 16:15, 30:11; I Cor.9:27; I Thess. 4:6; Heb. 12:5

DISCOUAGEMENT - I Kings 19:3; Neh. 4:10; II Tim. 4:9-11

DISOBEDIENCE - Gen. 2:17; Lev. 10:1; Num. 14.40-41, 20:12; Deut. 1:37, 28:46; I Kings 20:36; II Chr. 18:28; Ps. 81:11; Prov. 28:14; Jer. 42:20; Ezek. 7:27

DISRESPECT - II Kings 2:23-24

DIVORCE - Deut. 21:14, 24:1; Ezra 10:17; Isa. 50:1; Mal. 2:14; Matt. 1:19; 19:1-19; Mark 10:1-12; John 4:18; I Cor. 7:15

DOUBTS - I Kings 17:24; Job 40:2; Ps. 69:1-3, 73:3-5; Eccl. 9:4-6; Jer.15:18; Mal. 3:14-15; Luke 7:19-23; John 21:15-17; James 1-8

EMOTIONS - Ps. 13:1-5, 88:5, 140:1-11; Prov. 14:29; Lam. 1:12

ENCOUAGEMENT - Josh. 1:9; Ps. 27:2; 31:6, 35:11-16

ENEMIES - Ps. 27:2, 31:6, 35:1-16

ENVY - Gen. 37; Mark 7:20-23; James 3:13-4:10

FAILURE - Judg. 14:4; Ps. 106:7-43; Matt. 26:75; Mark 14:72; Luke 22:61-62

FAITH - Ps. 116:10; Isa. 10-24; Jer. 12:5-6; Hab. 2:3, 11; Zeph. 3:15; Matt. 11:3; John 14:12; I Peter 1:7

FALSE ACCUSATIONS - Job 19:29; 31:35

FEAR - Exod. 14:12; Ps. 140:1-11; Isa. 38:10-14; Matt. 8:26; Mark 4:40; Luke 8:37

FORGIVENESS - Gen. 33:4, 50:15-20; Matt. 18:35; Luke 11:4, 15:17-24; Acts 7:60; Eph. 4:32; Col. 3:13; II Tim. 4:16

GOSSIP - Ps. 94:20-23, 122, 125:3; Prov. 10:18-21. 29:18; Eccl. 8:2-6, 10:6; Acts 4:19; Rom. 13:1-7; Titus 3:1-2

GREED - Num. 11:33; II Sam. 12:8; I Kings 20:34; Micah 2:1-2; Hab. 2:5

GRIEF - Lev. 10:6; Deut. 34:8; Josh. 7:6-10; II Sam. 13:19; Esther 4:1-2; Ezek. 27:30

GUILT - Gen. 44:16; Exod. 204; Lev. 4:2, 16:20-22; Deut. 28:65; Job 25:4; Isa. 6:6-7

HATE - Ps. 31:6, 139:21-22

HUMILITY - I Sam. 15:22; II Kings 17:14; Ps. 25; 131:1-2; Prov. 30:2-3; Mark 9:33-37; Luke 2:9-12, 9:48, 14:11; John 13:14-15

HYPOCRISY - Ps. 26:4-5, 66:18; Prov. 15:8; Isa. 5:18-19; Jer. 17:10, 42:20; Amos 5:21-23; Matt. 23:15, 33; Mark 7:11; Luke 12:1; John 8:7; Acts 5:5-10

ILLNESS - II Kings 5:1, 7:3; II Chr. 16:121, 21:15; Job 2:7-8; Ps. 38:3, 103:3

INCEST - Gen. 4:17, 19:31-32, 35:22; Lev. 20:17; Deut. 27:22; II Sam. 13:13; Amos 2:7

INJUSTICE - Job 24:1-12; Ps. 140:12; Eccl. 8:14; Amos 1:9

INTERCESSION - Gen. 18:23-32; I Kings 8:33-51; Ezra 9:5-15; Dan. 9:3-19; John 17; Rom. 8:26-27, 31-34; I Tim. 2:1-2; James 5:16; Heb. 7:24-25; I John 2:1

JOB ATTITUDE - Prov. 18:9, 28:19; II Thess. 3:10

LAZINESS - Prov. 6:6-11; II Thess. 3:6-13

LONELINESS - Ps. 4:34, 102:6-7, 16-18

LYING - Exod. 1:19-20; I Sam. 21:2, 27:8-10; II Kings 10:19, II Chr. 18:22; Ps. 62:4; Jer.38:27; Acts 5:5-10

PAIN - Job 16:6, 33:19; Jer. 15:15-21; Hab. 1:3; Rom. 5:1-5, 8:28-39; Rev. 21:1-4

PATIENCE - Gen. 40:23; I Sam. 13:11; Ps. 27:14; Prov. 14:29, 21:12; James 5:7-11

PEACE - Ps. 85:10-11, 147:14; Eccl. 11:10; Isa. 11:6-9; Rom. 12:18

PERSECUTION - Ps. 118:6; Dan. 11:35; Matt. 5:11-12; Luke 6:29-30; Acts 7:51-53, 14:22; Phil. 3:10; II Thess. 1:4-5; I Peter 1:6; Rev. 7:14, 13:17

PESSIMISM - Eccl. 1:2

PREJUDICE - Gen. 43:32, 46:34; Esther 2:10; Amos 1:13; Jonah 4:3; Matt. 2:23; Luke 9:53, 20:16; John 4-9; Acts 6:1; I Thess. 2:16

PRIDE - II Kings 17:14, 20:13; II Chr. 32:25-26; Job18:2; Ps. 18:44-45, 25:9; Prov. 21:4; Isa. 16:6; Luke l7:7-10; I Cor. 5:2, 14:18; GaI.6:4

PROSTITUTION - Gen. 19:4-5, 38:15, 21; I Kings 14:24; Prov.7:4-5; James 2:25

PURITY - Lev. 6:10; Josh. 5:15; Mal.3:2; I John 3:3

RACISM - Exod. 1:9-10; Esther 2:10; Amos 1:13

RAPE - Gen. 19:8, 34:26; Deut. 22:19, 29; Judg. 19:24; II Sam. 13:13

REBELLION - Num. 15:30; I Sam. 15:22-23; Ps. 85:4, 107:11; Isa. 1:24, 57:17; Nahum 3:1-4; Acts 26:14; Rev. 16:6, 17:3

RECONCILIATION - Matt. 5:23-26; II Cor. 5:11-6:2; Eph. 2:11-22; Phil. 4:2-3; Col. 1:15-23

REJECTION - Ps. 88:14; John 9:22

REPENTANCE - Lev. 26:41; I Kings 21:27; II Kings 6:30; II Chr. 33:1-2; Ps. 79:8; Isa. 1:18; Joel 2:12-14

RESPONSIBILITY - II Kings 21:9; I Tim. 4:14

REVENGE - Exod. 21:23-25; Lev. 24:20; II Sam. 19:22; I Kings 2:6; Ps. 58:6-8, 94:1-3, 149:6-9; Jer. 46:10; Ezek. 25:3-7; Matt. 5:39; II Tim. 4:14

SHAME - Ezra 9:6-15; Ps. 25, 34:1-7;

SLANDER - Ps. 121:5; Prov. 10:18-21; James 4:11

SORROW - Exod. 31:1-9; Matt. 26:36-46

STEALING - Exod. 20:15, 22:1-15; Lev. 19:11-13; Mal. 3:8-10; Eph. 4:28

SUFFERING - Job 5:7, 6:24, 11:16, 34:37; Ps. 88:3; Mark 8:34, 15:23; Acts 5:41; Rev. 13:10

SUICIDE - I Sam. 31:5; II Sam. 17:23; Isa. 57:1-2; Acts 18-19, 16:22 36

TEMPTATION - Deut. 13:3; I Chr. 21:1; Job 29:2, 31:1; Ps. 81:7; Matt. 4:1,3,4; Mark 1:12-13; Luke 4:3; I Cor. 10:13; Eph. 6:14-17; Heb. 4:15; James 1:13; I John 5:4

UNBELIEF - Num. 10:12; Deut. 1:34; Ps. 78:32, 95:11, 115:2, Isa. 29:9-10; Matt. 12:39; Mark 6:5-6; Luke 11:29, 10:26

WAITING - Isa. 64:4; Amos 5:13; Hab. 2:1

WIDOWS - Deut. 25:5-9; Isa.4:1, 54:1-

6; Micah 2:9; I Tim. 5:9

WITCHCRAFT - Lev. 20:6-7; Deut. 18:10-12; I Sam, 28; Isa. 8:19-22, 47:10-14; Acts 8:9-24, 13:6-12, 19:13-19; Gal. 5:19-21

YOUTH - Eccl. 11:7-12:7; Joel 2:28-32; Acts 2:13-36; I Tim. 4:11-16

TRADITIONAL JEWISH SONGS

ADOM OLAM

Adom olam asher malach, b'terem kol y'tzir nivra L'et na'asah v'chef'tso kol, azai melech sh'mo nikra

V'acharei kich'lot hakol, levado yimloch nora

V'hu haya, v'hu hoveh, v'hu y'hiyouh b'tifara

V'hu echad v'ein sheini, l'hamshil lo l'hachbirah

B'li reishit b'li tachlit, v'lo ha'oz v'hamisrah

V'hu eili v'chai go'ali, v'tzur chevli b'et tzarah

V'hu nisi u'manos li, m'nat kosi b'yom ekrah

B'yado afkid ruchi, b'et ishan v'a-ira

V'im ruchi g'viyati, Adonai li, v'lo ira

Eternal Lord who ruled alone before creation of all forms, when all was made at His desire, then as the king was He revealed.

And after evening shall end alone, in wonder, will He reign, as once He was, so is He now, the glory that will never change.

He is the One, no other is to be compared, to stand beside, neither before, nor following, His is the strength and His is the might.

This is my God, my life he saves, the rock I grasp in deep despair, the flag I wave, the place I hide, He shares my cup the day l call.

Within His hand l lay my soul both when I sleep and when I wake, and with my soul my body too, my Lord is close I shall not fear.

EIN KELOHENU

Ein kelohenu, ein kadoneinu,
Ein kemalkeinu, Ein kemoshienu.

Mi kelohenu, mi kadoneinu,
Mi kemalkeinu, mi kemoshienu.

Nodeh lelohenu, nodeh ladoneinu,
Nodeh lemalkeinu, nodeh lemoshienu.

Baruch elohenu, baruch adoneinu,
Baruch malkeinu, baruch moshienu.

Atah hu elohenu, atah hu adoncinu,
Atah hu malkeinu, atah hu moshienu.

There is none like our God,
There is none like our Lord,

There is none like our King,
There is none like our Savior.

Who is like our God, Who is like our Lord?

Who is like our King, Who is like our Savior?

We give thanks to our God. We give thanks to our Lord,

We give thanks to our King. We give thanks to our Savior.

Blessed is our God, Blessed is our Lord,

Blessed is our King, Blessed is our Savior.

You are our God, You are our Lord,

You are our King, You are our Savior.

HINEI MAH TOV

Hinei mah tov u-mah na'im,
Shevet achim gam yachad
Hinei mah tov u-mah na'im,
Shevet achim gam yachad

Hinei mah tov u-mah na'im,
Shevet achim gam yachad
Hinei mah tov u-mah na'im,
Shevet achim gam yachad

Behold, how good and pleasant it is
for brethren to dwell together in unity.
Behold, how good and pleasant it is
for brethren to dwell together in unity.

Behold, how good and pleasant it is

for brethren to dwell together in unity.
Behold, how good and pleasant it is
for brethren to dwell together in unity.

L'CHA DODI

L'cha dodi likrat kala

P'nei Shabbat n'kabalah

(refrain)

Shamor v'zakhor b'dibur e-had

Hishmianu El ha-me'yuhad.

Adonai e-had u-sh'mo e-had

L'shem u-l'tiferet v'lithilah.

(L'kha dodi ...)

Likrat Shabbat l'khu v'nelkhah!

Ki hi m'kor habracha

Merosh mikedem n'sucha

Sof ma'aseh b'machshava t'chila.

(L'kha dodi ...)

Hitoreri, hitoreri

Ki va orech kumi ori

Uri uri shir dabeiri

K'vod hashem alayich nigla.

(L'kha dodi ...)

Yamin u-s'mol tifrotzi

V'et Adonai ta'aritzi

Al yad ish ben Partzi

V'nis m'ha v'nagilah.

(L'kha dodi ...)

Bo'i v'shalom ateret ba'la

Gam b'simcha uv-tzohola

Toch emunei am s'gula

Bo'i chala, bo'i chala.

(L'kha dodi ...)

Come, my friend, to greet the Bride

Let's encounter the presence of Shabbat.

(refrain)

Observe and remember in one word.
The One God who caused us to hear.
Adonai is One and the Divine Name is One.
To the Divine Name is the glory and the fame.
(refrain)

To greet the Shabbat, let us go!
Because it is the source of blessing,
Conceived before life on earth began.
Last in God's work, first in God's thought.
(refrain)

Arise, arise, for your light has risen,
For the dawn has broken, the light has come.
Awake, awake, and joyously sing;
The honor of Adonai is upon you and revealed.
(refrain)

From the right to the left, you will prosper;
And you will always revere Adonai.
Through the person descended from Peretz.
We will rejoice and exult.

(refrain)

Come in peace, crown of her husband,
Come in happiness and with good cheer.
Amidst the faithful of the treasured people,
Come, Bride; Come, Bride!
(refrain)

HATIKVA

(The Jewish national Anthem)

Kol-od ba-l'vav p'-ni-ma

Ne-fesh y'hu-di ho-mi-a ul'fa-a-te-miz-rach

Ka-di-ma a-yin l'tsi-yon tso-fi-a

Od lo av-da tik-va-te-nu

Ha-tik-va bat shnot al-pa-yim

li-yot am chof-shi b'are-tse-nu

e-rets tsi-yon vi-ru-sha-la-yim

li-yot arn chof-shi b'are-tse-nu

e-rets tsi-yon vi-ru-sha-la-yim.

As long as a Jewish heart beats, and as long as Jewish eyes look eastward then our two thousand year hope to be a free nation in Zion and Jerusalem is not lost.

BIBLIOGRAPHY

"Abodath Israel, A Prayer Book for the Services of the New Year at the Synagogue," Benjamin Szold and Marcus Jastrow, Rev, Ed, Philadelphia, 1914.

"High Holiday Prayer Book," Rabbi Morris Silverman, Prayer Book Press, Hartford, 1951.

"The Union Prayer Book of Jewish Worship, Part I." The Central Conference of American Rabbis, Cincinnati, 1918.

"The Union Prayer Book of Jewish Worship, Part II," The Central Conference of American Rabbis, Cincinnati, 1922.

"Gates of Prayer - The New Union Prayer Book,' Central Conference of American Rabbis, N.Y., 1975.

"Mahzor for Rosh Hashanah and Yom Kippur,"
Rabbi Jules Harlow, The Rabbinical Assembly, N.Y., 1972.

Ray Looker (1940 -   )

Biography

Ray Looker is a disciple of Yahshua the Messiah, an apostle of the Messianic faith and has been a Professor of Theology. Ray is committed to preparing the Church for the coming of the Messiah.

Ray spent 14 years in the U.S. Army as a Senior-Ranking Non-Commissioned Officer. His military assignments took him to Greenland, Germany, Norway and Vietnam. He served in seven major campaigns in Vietnam, and has spent over 30 years as a Missionary and Professor in Europe, China and the inner-cities of America.

With graduate degrees in Law, Ray worked as a Law Clerk in a Public Defender's Office and with a District Court Judge while doing post-graduate work for a Doctor of Theology Degree. His post-Doctorate research in Educational and Motivational Psychology in Finland allowed him to be a Program Manager in an epidemiological study of mental illness for the Department of Health and Mental Retardation for the State. He later served as a Director of Compliance enforcing a Federal Court Order on a maximum security prison for the criminally insane, a Justice of the Peace, a Notary Public and as an Auxiliary Police Officer in the State of New York.

Ray ran for the House of Delegates and as a Magistrate with the idea that government 'servants' were to be held accountable to the people for their actions. In addition Ray has also served as Pastor in a Christian Church and as a Messianic Rabbi in a Messianic Jewish Congregation. He has also ministered on both radio and television and has been a Baritone Soloist in various churches when asked to do so.

When the Messiah comes all men will be mandated to observe the Commandments of Yahweh: i.e. the Feasts of Yahweh, His Sabbaths, the New Moons, and the Dietary Laws of the written TORAH. Ray's work and ministry is to prepare and to teach Believers the importance of keeping Yahweh's laws and commandments in accordance with His wishes and desires for us.

To raise up the 'Tabernacle of David' in preparation for the coming of the Lord, the Church must rebuild and restore Christianity upon the bedrock foundation of the Apostles and Prophets, which is the written TORAH.

Ray's many books on Messianic Judaism are a testimony of the dedication of his life to preparing the way for the coming of the Messiah. As he is able, he intends to make these books available on the internet for worldwide access to everyone, everywhere.

~ DESCRIPTION OF ~
BOOKS BY RAY LOOKER

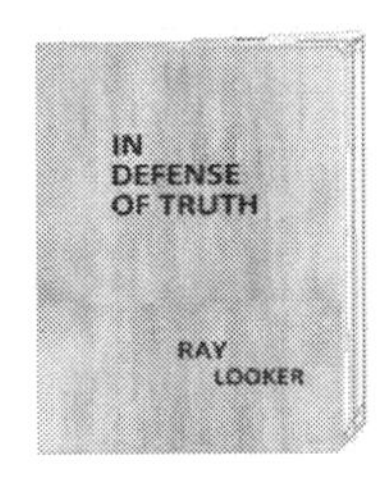

IN DEFENSE OF TRUTH

ISBN: 1480049735

Is truth relevant to salvation?

In a philosophical and theological approach "In Defense of Truth" challenges the validity of the traditions and practices of the Jewish, Christian and Catholic religions.

Is truth relevant to religious belief, or is the basis of salvation best achieved by deception, outright lies and religious myth?

The author uses the Bible as the basis and sole authority for determining the validity of tradition and practice.

Available: Amazon.com (Paperback and Ebook)

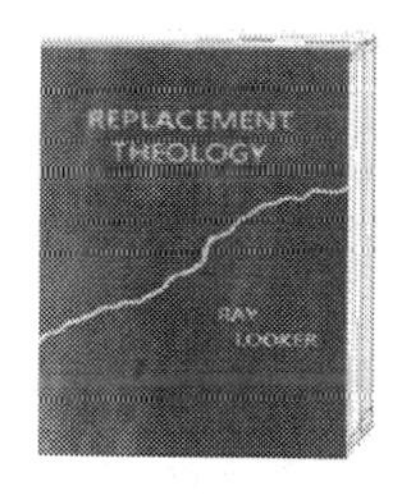

REPLACEMENT THEOLOGY

ISBN: 1480049506

A provocative challenge to the modern day practices of the Jewish, Christian and Catholic religions.

"Replacement Theology" reveals the subtle shift from the mandates of Scripture to the inclusion of pagan and manmade traditions and practices within each of these religions.

Herein is presented a concise revelation that threatens to overturn centuries of religious abuse and practice within each of these religions.

The source and foundation for these challenges lies in the Bible and what the God of Abraham, the God of Isaac, and the God of Jacob expects from each of us.

Available: Amazon.com (Paperback and Ebook)

JUDEO-CHRISTIANITY, 2ND Edition

ISBN: 1481906216

For almost two thousand years we have followed the traditions and practices of the Catholic religion.

But is this reflective of the Apostles and Prophets of Christianity?

Judeo-Christianity challenges these practices as being of pagan origin and invites us to rethink what we are doing in the light of the Scriptures.

The Catholic religion has dictated our traditions and practices to the extent that Christians are not following the teachings of the Bible. Judeo-Christianity provides solutions and shows how we can get back to the Bible in our practices and establish traditions that are in line with the will of God in our lives and in our Churches.

Available: Amazon.com (Paperback and Ebook)

MESSIANIC PRAYER BOOK, 2ND Edition

ISBN: 1481130692

This Second Edition of the Messianic Prayer Book has been greatly expanded in breath and scope.

The inclusion of transliterated Hebrew Blessings is designed to allow the reader to learn to pray the blessings in the Hebrew language.

The major emphasis of the Prayer Book is on family worship and the teaching of obedience to the Word of Yahweh to the next generation. The entire construct lends itself to increased family interaction, and quality time spent together in worship to Yahweh.

Available: Amazon.com (Paperback and Ebook)

YAHSHUA – THE MESSIANIC HOPE

ISBN: 1482701677

Yahshua - The Messianic Hope is a chronological presentation of the life of Yahshua the Messiah, which uses His Hebrew name, and eliminates the anti-Semitism that is present in the Gospels as written.

The story has been reconstructed using the Gospels as a guide in its presentation.

The narrative is written in modern English and makes for easy reading and provides a better understanding of His life and His mission.

The chronological presentation of the story clears up the events which began on His birth date on Tishrei 15, the first day of the Feast of Tabernacles and leads up to, and includes, His presentation in the Temple as the Passover Lamb on Nisan 10.

Available: Amazon.com (Paperback and Ebook)

MESSIANIC GUIDE TO THE EPISTLES

ISBN: 1480049840

This Messianic Guide to the Epistles challenges the authority of these commentaries on Scripture as presented by the Epistles, and explains more accurately what constitutes Scripture and what constitutes a commentary on Scripture.

Ever since the Catholic religion established the New Testament as the basis of both the Catholic and Protestant Churches, the Epistles have been the foundation for the development of tradition and practice for both Catholics and Protestants.

The Epistles have been used extensively as the authority for the interpretation and application of the New Testament, with tradition and practice of the Catholic religion assuming an even more central position of power. But is this a valid approach to the application of Scripture in our lives?

Available: Amazon.com (Paperback and Ebook)

MESSIANIC CODE OF JEWISH LAW

ISBN: 1481850172

The "Messianic Code of Jewish Law" is an adaptation of those aspects of Jewish Law which every believer should know and do.

Each law is based upon a precept is based upon how to observe that Mandate. Under the Messianic Covenant we have an enhancement of the concept of law administered in love.

The love of a father with a child expresses a new concept of legal administration not previously in evidence, but is expressed more specifically in the Messianic Covenant.

On the Day of Judgment everyone will be judged by the Laws of the written Torah. The Messianic Code of Jewish Law is primarily presented as a guide to help us be obedient to the Will and Commandments of God as revealed by Yahweh in the Bible.

Available: Amazon.com (Paperback and Ebook)

AMAZING GOSPEL OF JESUS

ISBN: 1490534911

For two thousand years the story of Jesus has been published and preached around the world.

The Gospels of Matthew, Mark, Luke and John were originally selected as New Testament Canon late in the Third Century among the Gentile Churches, and the name 'Jesus Christ' was incorporated therein to replace His Jewish name of 'Yahshua the Messiah'.

The story of Jesus is presented herewith and incorporates all the aspects of the Four Gospels as presented in the King James Bible and selected Scriptures from the Books of Acts and Revelation which reflect upon future events.

Available: Amazon.com (Paperback and Ebook)

SUFFERING FOR

RIGHTEOUSNESS SAKE

ISBN: 1492294551

The story of Job is explained with an application to the afflictions of righteous people who endure persecution; a message of hope for those who are being tested for their faith; a time of preparation for greater ministry and service for the Lord.

Available: Amazon.com (Paperback and Ebook)

END TIME PROPHECY

ISBN: 1494375516

A vivid description of prophecy, that is about to happen in the world.

As we come to the end of the age a new world government is about to ascend out of the pit which most Christians are not prepared to accept, nor have they prepared for the coming of the Messiah.

"End-Time Prophecy" alerts Christians to prepare or suffer the consequences of not being ready. This will be a time of suffering and persecution for both Jews and Christians far beyond anything the world has ever seen before.

The time to prepare is now. This is a message to the Church on what to expect and how to get ready.

Available: Amazon.com (Paperback and Ebook)

Made in the USA
Lexington, KY
14 April 2014